THE BOUNCEBACK:

FROM HEARTBREAK TO WHOLENESS

(W/ Enclosed Workbook)

Written by LisaBeth Willis

Abounding Phoenix Publishing, LLC

DEDICATION

The BounceBack: From Heartbreak to Wholeness is dedicated to the memory of my Cousin, Olivia Juanita Booker (Day). Affectionately known as "Tinky," her body was tired and she was called to Heaven while experiencing her own BounceBack. I am forever grateful for her love and support of this project.

It is also dedicated to my Aunt, Dorothy Thompson, the most beautiful, sassy eighty-five-year-old I have ever met. You were called to Heaven when I was still in the darkness, but oh, how I wish you were here to witness the healing and transformation. Thank you for loving me and for being a wonderful example of a wife (married sixty-two years) and a woman who maintained her own identity and independence.

Last, but not least, it is dedicated to Joanne Murphy, the mother of my youngest Brother Michael. When I sought respite from life's challenges in the mountains of North Carolina, you were a sounding board and a great consult at my darkest hour. Thank you and may you Rest in Heaven.

ACKNOWLEDGMENTS

Words cannot express my sincere gratitude for everyone who loved me in a season of life when I didn't love myself. Some of them were friends, teachers, mentors (known and unknown), and others who supported me over the years. First, I would like to thank my mother, Gladys Juanita Willis. Your unending support and love fuel me with the drive to succeed at all costs. Because of you, I know that I can succeed at anything. To my children, Christopher and Kierston (Katy), you two are my heartbeats, and my world is rich and full of love because you are in it. Thank you for being wonderful. To my siblings: Devedre Jo Slaughter, Darin Willis, Sheri Willis-Oninku (Jonas), Bayle Lael, and Michael Murphy (Kimberly), thank you all for imparting wisdom when I needed it most. Aunt Betty and Uncle Greg, your prayers have carried me through some of the darkest days I have seen. Thank you. Uncle Joseph and Aunt Saundra Edwards, you have been an incredible support. Special thanks to my father, Larry Edwards (deceased).

A special thank you to Pastor Jimmy and Michelle Washington (Phillips Temple CME Church) for your encouragement over the years, even when I was away. Also, Bishop & Pastor K. Edwin Bryant (Dwan), whose ministry at the Mt. Pisgah Baptist Church, God used to lift my spirit during my transformation and healing. Every time I was depressed or going through a challenge I found myself in the pews of Mt. Pisgah. Thank you for letting God use you. Mica Goosby (Darin), your support is also appreciated. Also, my late pastor, Elder Will D. Mack, Mother Orvetta Mack and the Christ Temple C.O.G.I.C. for providing my spiritual foundation. I would also like to send a special thank you to Angie and Rodney Christian, Carla and Reggie Hawkins, Debbie and Christopher Shaw, Debra and Eric Battle. You guys loved and supported us both through the roller coaster and imparted wisdom when we both needed it. Marsha Bonhart, thank you for your advice and wisdom during my ex-husband's media storm; you helped me navigate with class and dignity.

Dawn Wood, Shereece Holmon, Stacy Thompson, Tina Henry, Stacy Jackson, Juanita Michelle Darden-Jones and, again, Angie Christian, you guys are both family and friends whose support has withstood the test of time as we support one another through life's transitions. Thank you all for your loving patience and support. Special honor and thanks to my ninety-two and ninety-four-year-old family patriarchs: Buster Thompson and Andrew Dicky Thompson (Uncle Dicky).

Special thanks to my fitness trainers, Virginia Johnson and Simone Woodall, of Just Sweat Fitness, LLC. While I was on my BounceBack journey, I made the commitment to reinvest in personal training and these two ladies were tough, but produced results. I would also like to thank the Beautiful Shades of Brown Book Club, who not only participated in my focus group, but invited me into the club with open arms. I truly love the intelligent conversation that these ladies have added to my life. They are helping me grow and expand my thinking.

I would be remiss if I did not thank Barbara Crossett-Hoffemeir, Andrea Rice-Mack, Rosemary McCullough and the late Donald Mitchell. The four of you were the reasons I graduated from Miami University. Also, Dr. Cheryl Johnson, who taught me to love African-American Literature. I can't wait to publish fiction. Dr. Ron Scott, who taught me how to analyze film. It's been over twenty years and I still can't watch a film without analyzing for deeper meaning. Dr. Hugh Morgan, who taught me how to write effectively. Also, Dr. Howard Kleiman, who taught me the importance of laws in communication. I may just need a refresher course at some point. (smile) Thank you all.

To my writing and business mentors, Tressa Azarel Smallwood, Valerie Lewis Coleman and Dr. Karen Townsend, you ladies keep this sister on her toes. Words cannot express my gratitude for each of you. Thank you.

Also, to my amazing editor, Tenita Chantilly Johnson of So It Is Written, LLC, whose patience has been golden and her work ethic superb. It seemed as if "life" were throwing more darts than I thought I could handle, but you stood consistent with me in prayer and encouragement. Thank you.

To my Life Coach, Angel Richards, thank you for your transparent style of pushing women to be their best. God sent you to me when I needed it most, and ever since that connection my "peace, happiness and success" have become non-negotiable and my growth "unstoppable." Also, Chanelle Wilson, my EPT (Emotional Polarity

Technique) Practitioner, you reminded me that 'God did not create me to be small,' and in that moment, I began to remember myself. I always said by the time I was in my forties I would be teaching college and writing; well, I've taught several courses at a community college and now I begin the writing. May you be blessed.

To the men who were my teachers, thank you and God bless.

FOREWORD

If you're diabetic, your doctor recommends medicine, dietary changes and regular exercise to manage the disease's effects on your body. If your personal expenses far exceed your income, your financial planner develops a budget to reduce your debt, manage your spending and boost your savings to generate investments for future earnings. If you're spiritually disconnected, your pastor recommends prayer, reading your Bible and fellowship with people who overcame similar experiences to reignite your faith. But what do you do when life has shattered your heart, demolished your dreams and seized your joy? You do what LisaBeth Willis did: stop the bleeding, cauterize the wound and seek expert help!

Because I serve professional speakers and experts to magnify and monetize their message by publishing quality books, LisaBeth hired me to launch her publishing company: Abounding Phoenix. In the midst of public scrutiny, finding herself and protecting her family, she pushed through her personal storm to develop her writing savvy. She attended several Pen of the Writer conferences, assisted with promotions and contributed to my bestselling anthology,

The Wait of Success: How to Become an Overnight Success in 7,300 Days.

As we worked together to establish her business portfolio, LisaBeth sought professional help to address the personal matters. She put action with her faith to get holistic, life-changing, repeatable results. Whether you're in a place of heartbreak, wholeness or somewhere in between, LisaBeth has done the work to fix her life and her BounceBack message will help you transform yours.

If you need validation, I affirm that you are fearfully and wonderfully made. Everything you need to fulfill His intended purpose is already inside you...tap into your greatness. If you're waiting for permission, I authorize you to fall head-over-heels in love with every aspect of who you are: the good, the bad and the ugly. And if you are ready to do the work, I ask you to read this book to change the trajectory of your life.

Valerie J. Lewis Coleman, award-winning author, publisher and mentor

PenOfTheWriter.com, QueenVPublishing.com

The Bounce Back FROM HEARTBREAK TO WHOLENESS

TABLE OF CONTENTS

LISABETH WILLIS

PART ONE

It All Began When
I Betrayed Myself

"How in the world did I get here?" I asked myself as I laid down on the brown leather couch, which held me and my daughter, who was still developing inside my oversized belly. Although I wanted her, had planned for her and even prayed for her, the environment in which she would be born was certainly less than desirable. My husband and I were clearly headed for divorce. I didn't have a grain of hope or energy left to try to save the marriage. Both my OB/GYN and neonatologist had placed me on bed rest. My little girl was trying to enter the world a bit too soon.

Looking back, I am confident that it was my stress level that caused problems during the pregnancy. Even still, I was determined to deliver her into the world safely. As I lay there, day after day, night after night, in a deteriorating marriage, clinical depression became eminent. As time passed, I could no longer envision my future; all I could see was my past, who I used to be, and what I used to do. I remembered the vibrant girl I once was. The one who was full of passion for life. The one who networked her way into the music business in Chicago in the mid-nineties.

As a child, I had always loved music. I used to sing like I breathed. It filled me up; I sang every day, all day. In fact, the first song I learned was "Lean on Me," by Bill Withers. Not long thereafter, I heard the beautiful voice of Natalie Cole. Listening to her is where I learned that I not only could sing, but I wanted to be a singer. The songs that caught my ear were "I've Got Love on My Mind" and "Our Love." I even pretended to be Natalie as my cousin Anissa, (who preferred Donna Summer) and I performed from time to time at family gatherings. As I grew older I developed my "ear" for music and vocals singing in the church choir and listening to gospel groups like the Clark Sisters, the Winans and Commissioned. I also sang in a group with three other young ladies at church, we called ourselves

"Vision." Music to me was a gift that I not only recognized as a gift, but it was my opportunity to share with others.

Unfortunately, it wasn't necessarily something that I was encouraged to do at home. I was told that the music business wasn't "real" and like many other young African-Americans, I was told to 'go to college, so I could get a good job,' and that is exactly what I did. I graduated from one of the top universities in the Midwest and moved to Chicago from Ohio after earning my bachelor's degree and completing my master's degree coursework. Fortunately, I was hired to be Market Manager for the consumer division of the world's largest pharmaceutical company and relocated to the Windy City.

I was twenty-five when I relocated on July 5, 1995. Initially, when I began my job and got settled in, I was excited with my new lifestyle. Unfortunately, the excitement was short-lived. Over time, I wasn't fulfilled. I felt empty, as if something were missing. I just knew there had to be more to life. I went to church often, prayed and one day my answer came as I traveled my territory, which covered Ohio, Indiana and St. Lewis. I had been listening to cassettes by Motivational

Speaker, Tony Robbins. One of my key takeaways from this series, was when he stated that 'if you want to know who you were and what you should be doing, you should think back to your childhood and remember what you wanted to be when you 'grew up.' I embraced that thought and applied it to my life. I was born to be a singer, that was my God-given identity and talent. That was my truth, but I had no idea where to start; so, I prayed.

The following year, I moved downtown to the 25th floor of a high-rise apartment with a jaw-dropping view of beautiful Lake Michigan. I absolutely loved that apartment, but the people I met made the experience more amazing. One of the people I met was a motivational speaker, while another was a vocalist in town from New York who was working on a musical. I also met a producer from The Oprah Winfrey Show; I was in total awe. These people were living their dreams. It was very rare, in those days, to meet anyone living out their passions from day to day. Most people merely worked to make a living. Working one's dream job or career wasn't common.

One day while I was riding on the elevator, I met a man

who was not only on his path to purpose, but he believed in me and introduced me to the music industry. His name was Robert. Robert was a marketing and promotions manager for a record label and had relocated temporarily to Chicago. One day, he invited me to a listening party for Sean "Puff Daddy" Comb's new release. It was hot! All of Chicago's music industry insiders were there, and Robert knew exactly who to introduce me to for an initial industry opportunity. When we arrived, the ambiance was buzzing with people dressed in their expressive fashions. The walls vibrated with music as everyone bobbed their heads to Lil Kim's whispers on the track. By the time the verse came on featuring the Notorius B.I.G., it was a done deal. Everyone knew it was a hit. I was enamored with the whole scene.

Finally, Robert introduced me to Don, a former radio station programmer at the top R&B radio station in Chicago. Don was in the process of re-launching Public Announcement, the group in which megastar R. Kelly launched his career. Knowing how impulsive the industry was, I knew I had to be prepared for an impromptu performance. After the introduction, Robert told Don I could sing.

As I expected, Don said, "Okay, let me hear you." So, on the spot, I started singing in his ear. He said, "Okay, meet us at the studio tomorrow." When I arrived at the studio the next day, Don and the members of Public Announcement were already at work, putting final touches on one of their soon-to-be-released hits. It was an amazing experience. It was the first time I'd been in a real studio, especially in the company of professional artists. I later learned that Hinge Studios was the same place where Destiny's Child recorded the remix for "No, No, No" with Wyclef Jean. My dream was becoming tangible; it was really happening.

After the session, Don met with me and I shared with him all the research I'd conducted on the industry. I wanted him to know that I was not only hungry for success, but also well-studied. I elaborated on the different types of copyrights, I talked about publishing and the importance owning your own publishing, etc. The funny thing is that I talked so much that I impressed Don more with my book knowledge than my vocal talent. As I got to know him, I learned that he had great instincts. He knew talent when he saw it. He knew that while I could sing well, my stronger talent was business sense. He was also the first to recognize me as a writer, outside of an educational setting. He ultimately hired me in a consultant role as his executive assistant. Over the next year, I worked as a liaison between Don's production company, Unohoo Entertainment, and his label partner, A&M Records.

In that role, I was Don's right hand. I took care of administrative duties, took calls, assisted the travel agent with schedules, and even attended a few music conferences. Watching the magic of music come together in the studios and meeting lots of fascinating people were sheer bonuses. I met Jodi Watley at a conference in San Diego. She was the only artist that had me "star struck." She was very classy and at the top of the game in the late 1980s and early 1990s. She was rebooting her career after taking a break to raise her family. During her sabbatical, Janet Jackson had pretty much taken over the R&B and pop music scenes; Brandy and Monica were heavy on her heels. I met other amazing artists as well; however, it was nothing like my encounter with Jodi Watley. In fact, I still have the autographed calendar from that chance meeting.

At one point, I caught a glimpse of Aaliyah (RIP) while

walking through the hall of a hotel at a conference. I've always loved her. I wish the world could have experienced what the future held for her artistry. I also met R. Kelly and R&B legend, Roger Troutman. Roger and I were both from Hamilton, Ohio, and I used to live down the street from his parents on Washington Street. I often played with one of his nieces. Many people think he's from Dayton, but he is originally from Hamilton. He later moved to Dayton, which, after all, is the home of funk music. I met Roger when he came to Chicago to lend the touch of his famous voice box to the song "D. O. G." by Public Announcement. I also had the honor of meeting the original Destiny's Child members; they were only about seventeen years old at the time. The group had recently launched on the national scene. They were very giddy and their eyes beamed with excitement. I also saw LL Cool J in the airport, and my mouth literally watered as I witnessed his sexy muscles bulging beneath his jogging suit. When he smiled at me, and those dimples deepened as his beautiful pearly white teeth emerged... oh my God! Why couldn't he be single? I also saw Big Pun (RIP), Ice-T, Foxy Brown, and renowned DJs Tom Joyner and Doug Banks (RIP). Those were the days of my twenties, and I cherish those memories. I hold them very close to my heart.

The Unohoo Entertainment team was like a family. We all worked hard, but we had a lot of fun. Public Announcement released their first single, "Body Bumpin," which went Platinum. The album later went gold. After the hustle and bustle of the first project was over, things slowed down. Don and I agreed that it was time for him to streamline. There just wasn't enough work to justify keeping me onboard full time. Even though Public Announcement was back in the studio writing and recording, the other acts that were signed weren't quite ready for the next level. Neither was I.

Don always supported me. He encouraged me to push. He even came out to see me at an open-mic night. Don had it right when he said, "You're a writer." Back then, I kept a pen in my hand, drafting lyrics for potential songs. Of course, I wasn't fully ready to receive that. I had the stage in mind, but he was right. He had tremendous instinct. I was writing and copyrighting all the time. I knew the rules of publishing and the importance of owning your work.

I was very fortunate that he gave me that extraordinary opportunity, but from a financial perspective, it was time to move forward. Don was like a big brother to me, and I am forever appreciative for the insight on the industry and experience I gained while working on his team.

While I was working at Unohoo, I also worked from time to time as an "extra" on film sets, like Hoodlum and The Negotiator. I wanted to be a star. I knew, at some point, I would have to move to New York. It was the only way to further my artistic development and to expand my industry contacts. I wasn't quite ready yet, though. I loved Chicago, and I didn't want to leave my friends and business relationships I'd built. But I needed to get a job. Fortunately, I had a Plan B, which was to utilize my education and go back to Corporate America.

In the fall of 1998, I left the production company and joined a consulting firm to do Y2K remediation work on IBM's AS400 system. I worked on a pilot project with a diverse team of ten people from all racial and career backgrounds, which exemplified the ability to build and maintain professional relationships. We were vigorously trained on how to make system changes, but our primary job was to build and develop customer relationships, upon which the overall business could be expanded. While technically gifted people sometimes lack the ability to connect with people on an interpersonal level, communication was a natural gift for me. Learning the technical aspects of the job was extremely challenging, but somehow, I made it.

As the world approached December 31, 1999, concern grew into anxiety as everyone became afraid that when clocks struck midnight on that eerie New Year's Eve, computer systems all over the world would fail. Scientists and engineers weren't sure if planes would be able to fly, if there would be power outages, or if the world's communication systems would go completely black. It was a very intense time. People everywhere stocked up on water, clothes and non-perishable foods, just in case the world erupted in chaos. Following training, and after a week "on the bench," I was placed on a project in Calgary, Alberta, Canada. Once a month, I flew to Calgary with my team. We worked during the day and, in the evening, engaged in dinner and conversation with clients. After several months, the project was complete. I was then placed with a new

Chicago-based client.

After nine months, that project ended and my whole team was dismantled. Fortunately, we were told we could keep our jobs until we found other employment. At that point, I was confident that I was ready for New York, but I needed to save money and, quite frankly, I missed my family. After faxing my resume, I received a call three days later for an interview. Two weeks later, I was hired into the pharmaceutical industry with another mega giant. Within a month, they moved me to Cincinnati and a week later, I flew to Philadelphia to begin my nine-week training program. I studied more in those nine weeks than I studied in my whole college career, undergrad studies and graduate school combined. I had to pass every exam with 90% with only twenty-four hours to study huge scientific manuals. It was difficult, but I was successful.

Following training, I returned to Cincinnati and reconnected with a gentleman I met in graduate school years before. Eventually, I became the mother of his child. New Year's Eve and Y2K were uneventful, as many citizens watched television to see how moving into the Millennium affected the world globally. From New Zealand to Australia, Japan, China, and all the countries in between, there was absolutely no sign of computer failure related to the "Year 2000" of which I am aware. Looking back, the whole experience was quite hilarious, especially considering that nothing happened at all. Nevertheless, it was the state of the world at that time. It was a time of total uncertainty. It was also a time of uncertainty for me as I entered uncharted territory. I had no idea that God had motherhood planned for me. I wasn't ready and I was shocked, but I moved forward with the pregnancy. I accepted that I had to delay New York a few more years.

My son, Christopher, was the most beautiful baby I had ever seen. He was handsome and charming, just as he is today. However, he had challenging respiratory issues that kept us in and out of the hospital for the first two years of his life. After caring for him and ensuring that he was fully stable, I turned my focus back to my dreams. When he turned three, I began the transition by resigning from my corporate position. I hit the road for trips to New York for auditions and movie "extra" work. I also looked for a daycare. I embraced the overall lifestyle of New Yorkers. It was time to pursue what I wanted.

My mom agreed to keep Christopher until I was settled. I had music industry contacts in place, and I agreed to sublet my best friend's apartment in Brooklyn. I began the audition process and chose the acting school where I would hone my skills. One trip proved to be more impactful than I originally thought for several reasons. I was an extra on the HBO hit series The Sopranos and I auditioned for the Broadway play Hairspray. I gave show business my last shot. I was hungry and thirsty for the industry that I had longed for all my life.

However, the evening after the audition, Christopher had a conversation with my mother, in which he expressed his need to be with me. My mother so eloquently relayed the message: "Meemaw, I keep telling my mommy to come home, but she won't." My heartstrings were being pulled by my heartbeat. Although my son had only been in the world for three years, other than my relationship with God, he had become the very reason for my existence. My mind was racing in a million directions. There I was, thirty-three years old in New York City, where I truly felt free and believed that anything was possible; it was in the air. As I walked through the streets and encountered strangers, I received confirmation that I was on the right path; I felt the welcome. Many people saw me and would say, "Who are you? You are somebody; are you an actress or singer?" This was my destiny, and I was living it out. My life was fully aligned for the first time in years.

I was also fully aware of the unwritten rules in the industry when it came to looks and age. Like most African-Americans, due to the melanin in my skin, I looked relatively young. At that time, I could easily "pass" for being in my twenties. However, the reality was that I was a mother. I still owed my son the best life possible. I knew he was a gift from God. I just had to give him my very best.

"Tell Chris I will be there tomorrow." I woke up the next morning at 4:30, packed my things, and did not return to New York for nine years. I didn't pray first. I didn't ask God one question, nor did I meditate. Out of emotion, I decided to return home without consultation from anyone, not even my closest cousin, Stacy. Stacy had been my prayer partner through almost every major decision in my adult life. In fact, leaving New York went fully against the step of faith I'd taken to begin my journey.

After passing through the Holland Tunnel, I stopped in Newark, NJ to purchase gas. My intuition led me to look at a tire and, to my surprise, there was a huge bubble on the side of it. If I didn't have it changed, it was surely going to explode on the drive home. I had it fixed immediately and drove back to normalcy. It was then that I stepped out of the trajectory of my dreams and my purpose by making that one emotional decision. It changed everything. I didn't pray about it. I made the decision on impulse. I just got up and left. After all, it was for my son. How could I give him my best when I was miles away in a city where I had a limited support network? My lifestyle necessities were in place for me in New York, but not for him. Therefore, I walked away. This was the beginning of my spiral downward.

As I drove, I finally had a conversation with God, "Lord, if I can't have this, at least please let me get married." This was the only prayer I said on my way back to Ohio from New York. It was made purely based on emotions. I let go of my dreams and passions for what I considered a normal life.

My mind traced all the years that I longed to be in the entertainment industry, but was never encouraged to pursue it as a career. It wasn't until I reached my mid-twenties, after graduating from college, that I had the confidence to make it happen. I always had the burning desire to express my creativity. Music was always in my spirit and I just couldn't shake it. I remembered the family gatherings and singing the songs of Natalie Cole. I remembered it all, I remembered who God created me to be, but at that point I was also a mother, and my son needed me. Of course, I could have stayed in New York and moved forward with my plan, but that would've required faith and quite frankly the easy route was safer in my mind. So, I left "myself" on the drive home from New York.

After settling back in Ohio, I worked as a substitute teacher at a charter school and became an adjunct English instructor at a local community college. After a while, I resumed my career in pharmaceutical sales and settled into my regained "new normal." I had no idea of the importance of listening to that burn that God placed inside me. That hunger for more, that drive that no one else could quench. It seemed like I was doing the responsible thing, but at what cost? Time later revealed the cost and the alternatives that could have been chosen to keep me whole and responsible.

I started dating a gentleman whom I had met several years earlier. He was nice and intelligent, with a sort of quirky personality. Up until then, most guys I was interested in looked like professional athletes, with rock hard bodies chiseled straight from the gym, models from the cover of GQ magazine, or just regular, clean-cut men who possessed a style and coolness that exuded confidence. Contemporary urban culture refers to it as swag. "John" wasn't my typical kind of guy, but my life had changed so my dating decisions, I figured, had to follow suit. I chose to date the smart, confident (some called him arrogant) nice guy who proved he was my friend. He had strong family values and he lived with purpose. He knew who he was and had his own goals. That was very appealing.

John was different and, for me, different was a good thing, especially since my typical type had turned out to be undercover bad boys who often lacked maturity. This guy became my friend and, unbeknownst to me, would support me later in the loss of my father. My father, who resided in North Carolina, became ill in 2004. Although I didn't grow up in the same household with him, we grew closer over the years of my adult life. Unfortunately, during the time of his illness, I had no idea how bad off he was until it was almost too late.

After two months of getting to know John, my father passed away. John supported me through the process. Before long, we became a couple, regardless of various personality differences. He was a bit materialistic for my taste, so of course he didn't hold back when it came to wining and dining me. However, his commitment to his family and love for his community gained my attention more than anything. It's the intangible things that matter most to me. Material things can be fleeting and make for a weak foundation. Of course, I like nice things like everyone else, but it's not a driving factor in my life. I'm much more dangerous in a bookstore than I am in a department store. I could spend hours in bookstores, browsing, exploring and ultimately purchasing items outside of my planned budget, only to arrive home later with buyer's remorse. I could care less about fashion labels and popular style trends.

John was the total opposite. He had to wear Ralph Lauren clothing. He bought me purses with names like Dooney & Burke and Louis Vuitton, and the jewelry was almost always David Yurman. At one point, I was contemplating whether or not I wanted the relationship long-term. My cousin advised me, "Lisa, you better love the one that loves you." That was all I needed to hear. She was right. The guy I'd dated before him wasn't exactly marriage material, nor was he the best example for my son. John, on the other hand, appeared to be a gentleman. He wanted to love me and settle down. Over time, he worked hard to keep my interest and eventually I yielded. Having experienced what I believed to be more than my fair share of failed relationships, I told John that I would date him exclusively for one year. After that, I would make myself available to other suitors. Looking back, I'm not sure if it was fair to add that sort of pressure on anyone. At the time, though, I was tired of 'being the bridesmaid and not the bride.' I wasn't going to waste my time if it wasn't going anywhere. John, being the man he was, proposed and, nine months later, we married.

After the proposal, several events occurred that could easily have been interpreted as red flags, but neither of us chose to take note. Looking back, these incidents were also signs of me slowly losing my identity. The first incident was when my four-year-old son's older half-brother was tragically killed by a drunk driver the night of his college graduation. It was truly horrific for his dad and family, and they deserved support from both my fiancé and me. I was stunned when, instead of John lending support, he met me with an ultimatum when I informed him of the accident. He threatened to call off the engagement if I went to the funeral.

The person I am today would have walked away immediately from anyone with that level of insecurity; however, "Lost Lisa" sought advice to get through that situation. I phoned a trusted minister, who offered me wisdom that I will never forget. He said, "Lisa, you are about to marry a man who knows no compromise. The question is, 'Can you handle that?'" While I appreciate his words now, the reality is that's not what I wanted to hear at that time. I wanted someone to 'save' me by telling me exactly what to do. A healthy marriage and compromise go hand-in-hand; you can't have one without the other. I see it so clearly now but, back then, I didn't get it. As silly as it was, I didn't go to the funeral, however, I did send my son.

The other red flag was centered around our very first real argument. It took place in a Macy's store while we were completing our gift registry. When selecting our china pattern, I chose a beautifully decorated set that I liked versus a brand name that offered me nothing. In John's opinion, it had to be Lenox because "everyone" has Lenox because it's best in quality. I honestly didn't know anything about china or the quality of brands of china at the time. Not to negate or promote the quality of the Lenox brand or any other, the reality was I wanted something that I liked. After the disagreement, that lasted way too long and got a little too loud, just enough to cause brief attention from close onlookers, I relented to keep the peace. Again, this was a mistake. Chip, chip, chip. I was slowly giving myself away. This was the china pattern that we were choosing for my wedding. I was the bride. Most men don't even care about china. I should have stood my ground and stayed true to what I wanted. After all, it was my wedding. If he wanted to "win" this conversation without any pushback, a wiser approach would have been to have the salesperson educate us both on china patterns, quality and brands. His stance that we had to choose Lenox because of others' opinions wasn't impressive at all. I've never governed my decisions based upon popularity.

It didn't take long after the wedding for me to realize that our union wasn't exactly a match, although I don't recall any of those particular issues showing up while we were dating. John was a good guy with observably good intentions. However, disconnects in the most vital areas of marriage made it impossible for us to remain together for what we thought would be a lifetime. In fact, three weeks into the marriage, I knew intuitively that something wasn't quite right.

At the time, I hadn't fully learned to listen and obey God's Spirit. I know now that I should always heed my inner voice to avoid conflict. John and I differed in the most vital areas of marriage. My former husband and I simply did not speak the same love language, as Gary Chapman so eloquently puts it. Our differences were as opposite as Japanese is to English. We were totally foreign to one another. We didn't see eye to eye on money, communication or affection. These three areas encompass the leading cause of divorce nationwide. I knew if things didn't change, we would join 50% of Americans who divorce annually. Neither of us were perfect; we were just different. He is a spender, and I am more frugal. I am a communicator and I believe in talking out issues as they arise. John believes that things will work themselves out. I am highly affectionate and expressed my love accordingly. John showed his love by buying material gifts. We were truly night and day. There was no way we were going to make it. However, neither of us believed in divorce. We wanted commitment and marriage. Personally, I also didn't want to confuse my then five-year-old son.

As time passed, John transitioned into a political career and I continued in the pharmaceutical business. However, unlike First Lady Michelle Obama, when I was in the "political wife" role, I felt totally out of place. It wasn't that I didn't fit in, or couldn't handle the mix-and-mingle conversation with his political peers. I had my own education and mental capacity. I held my own. However, I wasn't true to myself. I wasn't living out my divine purpose, utilizing the gifts that God instilled within me. Oftentimes,

I sat quietly. I lacked passion for life. Not only had I stepped away from my goals, but I was in an unfulfilled marriage. I forgot who I was and attached myself to my husband's purpose. I was merely a guest on his path. I let my dreams go on the drive home from New York and, over time, I became a woman I didn't recognize. I took care of everyone, except myself. My creativity was at an all-time low as motivation drained from my spirit. I felt empty and lacked confidence as I poured myself into supporting my family. Everyone appeared to be happy, except me.

In the first year of my marriage, I went from a size eight to a size twelve. The deeper he embraced politics and public service, the more uncomfortable the marriage became. I looked for answers outside of myself to soothe the emptiness in my soul. During that phase of my life, I was so unsure of myself that I couldn't find my own spiritual center. I couldn't listen and follow my own intuition. My two closest cousins, "Starr" and "Denise" were always there when I called. These women believed in prayer, and they believed in marriage. Starr is my second cousin, but is only five years older than me and twenty-four years younger than my mother, who was her first cousin. Although I knew her my whole life, we became closer following my college graduation and relocation to Chicago. She had graduated from Spelman years earlier and lived there with her mother for over ten years. At that point, I hadn't seen Starr since I was fifteen. Denise's mom told me to make sure I called Starr as soon as I got to Chicago. My nerves got the best of me, and I waited at least a week before I phoned. After that call, we grew close as sisters. She became a confidante, a mentor and an advisor of the truth, even when I didn't want to hear it. Her favorite line to me in my "formative" twenties and early thirties was, "Tell your jokes to other folks. I know you." We're probably more alike than either of us would admit.

During the dark days of my marriage, Starr encouraged me to stand up and to stop hiding in my ex-husband's shadow. She'd always known me to be confident, outspoken and outgoing. She didn't recognize this "new Lisa" and it frustrated her to watch my personality dissipate. She reminded me that I was, "the cracker in that Cracker Jack Box." She pushed me to shine, even though my perspective was dim. Starr wasn't about to watch me stay down without fighting for me to get it together. She never told me what to do; she only asked questions and encouraged me to go deep within for the answers. I will forever love and appreciate her for reminding me of who God made me to be. She encouraged me to do the necessary work to get on track.

Denise and I are only nine months apart, and our mothers were sisters. Denise had always been a rock, steady and sure. She just listened. She was my sounding board. Oftentimes, we joked that she was "the vault." She held it all, without judgment, and every now and then offered a question or played devil's advocate. Over the years, we've supported each other through life's challenges. I truly value solid relationships, especially family.

Sometimes, there are things that occur in a marriage and God will not only understand if you divorced, but He, via the Holy Spirit and obvious signs, will encourage you to do so. There were times in my marriage when everything inside of me screamed for me to leave, and I stayed. However, I have no regrets. It wasn't all him, and it wasn't all me. The experience wasn't all bad. We were friends from day one. We both liked to be on the go, going to the movies, concerts, formals and sporting events. We had a lot of fun. Then, we experienced the exciting political exposure during the most important election in history. We took several trips to the Ohio Governor's mansion for events hosted by Governor and Mrs. Strickland. Then came President Obama's campaign. I had the pleasure of seeing him speak three times and I shook his hand twice. I had a lengthy chat with Michelle Obama on an occasion in Cincinnati. When the election was over, John, my son, and I travelled to Washington, D.C., where we witnessed the inauguration of the first black President of the United States of America. How proud we all were as we stood in the crowd of millions of Americans supporting that historic occasion!

In July of 2009, I became pregnant with our daughter. The following month, some of my paternal family members and I organized a Disney trip and rented a home in Orlando. While I fully enjoyed the vacation with my family, it was obvious to the rest of the family that my marriage was in trouble. Little to my knowledge, both of my uncles and aunts noticed the strained interaction between John and I. One night, John even slept on the couch. It was clear that things had gotten worse over time. We couldn't even hide it on vacation for a few days. One morning, my uncle approached me and asked if everything was okay, that he'd seen John sleeping on the couch the night before. My uncle, being an old-school southern gentleman who had been married for over thirty years, replied, "That's not normal. No matter what I deal with during the day, as a man, I look forward to getting home and laying in the bed next to my wife." What could I say to that? He was right. My marriage wasn't normal. We had more issues than not, and I was six weeks pregnant.

From Orlando, we drove to Destin, Florida, for John's cousin's wedding. On the way, we had a major argument, which ended with me telling him I was going to call an attorney and file for divorce. The stress of a deteriorating marriage eventually caused me to have numerous problems during the pregnancy. One night, I woke up and felt feeling dampness on the sheets. At first, I thought I might have somehow used the bathroom on myself. I reached under the sheets and it was totally wet. I raised the sheets and was shocked to see that I was lying in a puddle of blood. I screamed out for John, who rushed me to the hospital. They ran tests and, thankfully, the baby appeared to be normal. Doctors placed me on bed rest for three days. By the time I was four and a half months, problems continued. One evening at a church revival, I started having contractions which were ten minutes apart. Ironically, the next morning, I had an appointment scheduled to see my attorney. It was obvious that there was absolutely no way I could move forward.

When I arrived at the doctor the next day, my OB/GYN had been called into a delivery room for a birth. Almost an hour later, one of his partners examined me and discovered that I was one centimeter dilated. She sent me down the hall to the perinatal clinic, where I was told that I would be placed on bed rest for the remainder of the pregnancy. The doctor's statement caused me to go into an emotional tailspin. My marriage was already in trouble. I wanted out. But, how in the world was I going to leave when I knew my baby could be put at risk? I had no other option but to stay and pray for a healthy delivery.

The following months consisted of weekly exams at the perinatal specialist's office, weekly steroid injections by a home health nurse, and several procedures. In addition, I was diagnosed with gestational diabetes. Total anguish filled my mind as I lay on the couch, day after day, night after night, watching the world pass me by. I spoke with my pastor, who gave me a Scripture to read daily to proclaim victory over my challenges and to increase my faith.

I cried a lot and watched my favorite movies over and over. *Tyler Perry's Meet the Brown's* made me laugh, but also gave me hope. Then, there was *The Family that Preys*. At the end of the movie, Alfre Woodard's character drives off into the sunset as Gladys Knight's rendition of Lee Ann Womack's "I Hope You Dance" plays during the credits. That scene always made me cry because I felt as though my best days were behind me. In my mind, happiness was not in my future. I just could not see *forward*. My conversations were about what I used to do and who I used to be. I was only thirty-nine years old, but all I could see was my past.

My pregnancy continued to progress positively, while my marriage simultaneously continued to disintegrate. By the time I reached my seventh month, I weighed 180 pounds and verbal communication in the home was very limited.

It was time to make some decisions. I packed clothes for a week and called my mother to move my son and I in for a while so that I could have respite. Later that week, on the visit to the specialist, we discovered that a miracle had occurred. My daughter, who had been growing very low in my uterus, moved back to her proper position. It was truly amazing. I viewed it as a sign from God. I needed to stay away from the stress so that the remainder of my pregnancy would be healthy.

One day, my sister "Shanice" came by my mother's house after work with a note. She said it was from her co-worker, Shannon. The note held the Scripture from **Joel 2:25: So I will restore to you the years that the swarming locust has eaten, the crawling locust, the consuming locust, and the chewing locust, my great army which I sent among you.**

I wasn't sure what it meant to my life at the time because I hadn't lost anything. In fact, although I was seriously considering divorce, and had even threatened it, the truth was that I was still contemplating. I hadn't made any final decision. Nevertheless, I read it and put it away. Shannon was a Christian young lady who had recently gone through divorce. I now see her as an angel in disguise, whom God sent to encourage me. She even came to visit me during one of my hospitalizations.

I stayed with my mother until a week before my scheduled Caesarean section, then I returned to the marital home. When I reached my eighth month, my doctor removed me from bed rest. I knew that, despite the many conversations I had with people who encouraged me to stay in my marriage, my heart and spirit were truly done. I also knew that God understood my decision. I prayed my way out of my marriage. I didn't just get up and leave because things weren't going my way. I worked, communicated, tried and I fought hard--to no avail. When it became apparent that nothing I said or did made a difference, I knew it was time to leave.

After my daughter was born, I went home, allowed my body to heal, and settled into caring for our new infant. "Kalise" had finally arrived after almost five months of bed rest, which included three hospitalizations—the longest of which turned into a three-week stay. Not long thereafter, I returned to work and moved out for good with the children.

Beyond a shadow of a doubt, it was the best decision for everyone, even though the divorce got a bit ugly. I have no regrets. Before it was all over, God blessed us with a beautiful baby girl. Having her in my life now somehow made it all worth it.

Following the divorce, I told my friends, "I'm going to take a break. I'm not going to date anyone for three years. I'm just going to love on Lisa again and focus on my kids." I believed it when I said it; however, I did exactly the opposite. Feeling lonely after remaining faithful in a marriage that lacked the affection I needed, it wasn't long before I entertained telephone calls that I would've otherwise ignored. My three-year dating hiatus was reduced to one year. A man, whom I met five months after the initial separation, made it clear that he wanted to be in a relationship. I thought I was ready and fully healed. I now know that, even though a full year had passed, I hadn't fully healed from the marriage. I wasn't ready to begin a new love life. I hadn't regained my sense of self. Years of remaining in an unhealthy marriage had reduced my self-esteem to next to nothing. I didn't feel beautiful and I didn't feel loved. But, after a year of getting to know "Doug", we moved forward.

Doug was a communicator like me. He enjoyed having fun, deep conversations about issues that mattered. It's interesting because, on the surface, I wasn't even physically attracted to him at first. He was 'too smooth' for my taste. He was the ever-popular pretty boy. In fact, looking at younger pictures of him, he could have easily been mistaken for Pop and R&B sensation El Debarge. Over the course of a year, we laid a solid foundation of friendship without the complications of sex and expectations. It was totally platonic. With him, I could be free. I could be myself. Doug never tried to change me, and he knew the importance of compromise. He was the only guy I had dated that I could truly be uninhibited with, without fear of judgment. He's the only man who saw me at my worst. Over time, our friendship grew into love and passion. While I truly loved my ex-husband John, something about Doug was different. A friend mentioned that it wasn't that the relationship with Doug was so wonderful or different; he was simply what I needed at the time. As I reflect upon the experience, I think, perhaps, she was right.

Doug and I started out in the most innocent way possible; however, some areas of the relationship were as toxic as cyanide. We were both Virgos and we were both overthinkers. Although we like to think we are perfect, we are as flawed as any other human being. We are, by nature, highly analytical and sometimes overanalyze things. We sometimes focus on the wrong things so much that we create problems that don't exist. I can't say that for sure about all Virgos, but Doug and I were two of a kind in that department. Where we differed was that I have always been an incredibly decisive person and loyal, to a fault. He could sometimes be indecisive, which could be frustrating. Emotionally speaking, he shouldn't have been in a relationship either because his own personal experiences left him just as broken as I was.

Doug and I were not perfect. We loved each other but, over time, it grew into a level of co-dependence. In the beginning, we had fun and truly enjoyed one another's company. One of my favorite memories was a trip to the Motown Museum in Detroit with our besties, "Ricky" and "Annette", who were dating at the time. Our relationship was fresh and new, and we were beginning to make our own memories. It was exciting to be in the place where musical legends were made and contemporary R&B was born. To stand in the studio where The Temptations, Diana Ross, The Jackson Five, Smokey Robinson and The Miracles, The Four Tops and others recorded and wrote history, was amazing.

We booked our hotel rooms at the MGM Grand and had dinner at Wolfgang Puck. After dinner, as the waitress placed dessert on the table, Annette was greeted with a beautiful diamond engagement ring as she lifted the dessert plate cover. Doug was in on the surprise, but Annette and I were totally in the dark. It was beautiful as Ricky proposed and Annette embraced him as she said, "Yes!" Later that night, the four of us danced the night away at the club in the hotel.

As Doug and I settled into our relationship, we continued to discover one another and new ways to have fun. We often sang impromptu duets since we both loved to sing, he had a beautiful voice. A special favorite was Luther Vandross and Cheryl Lynn's song, "If This World Were Mine." We also took road trips to visit my family in Washington, D.C., and North Carolina. We enjoyed the many concerts and holidays we shared with our family and friends. After Ricky and

Annette's wedding, the whole "crew" was married, except for Doug and I. The heaviness of our individual issues was just too much strain on our relationship to develop into a lifetime. His Virgo analytical trait made him overthink even the smallest relationship challenges. My issues were based on my own insecurities due to drastic changes in my personal life.

People often say, "Life happens." Well, "life" happened to me at the very beginning of my relationship with Doug. I'm quite confident it didn't help our situation. Within the first month of our commitment, I was informed that I had to have major surgery. This led me to be on short-term disability from work for eight weeks; however, I loved my job so I decided to come back a week early. Unfortunately, my return also coincided with the company announcing a major downsizing. After surviving three such cuts, it was my turn. I was one of over 1200 representatives downsized globally that year. Up until that point, I'd been fortunate for the most part in my career. I'd never been downsized. For my industry, that was becoming extremely rare.

That experience was very difficult. I'd been with the

company for eight years and had assisted others along the way. In fact, I had just received a promotion prior to being placed on bed rest. At first, I was confident I would find something quickly because my resume was stellar; however, the whole industry was in a trouble. All the major pharma companies seemed to downsize at the same time. Positions were extremely limited in 2012. In the midst of transition, I remained diligent in my search. One month became three months, and three months became six months. My confidence took a deep dive as I questioned God and I embraced my 'inner victim.' During that time, my insecurities added pressure to the relationship that neither of us was prepared to handle. Doug's personal issues made him ill-equipped to love me through my challenges. Yet, my lack of inner security made me clingy and desperate for attention, in a way that was weak and foreign to me.

Finally, in the seventh month of unemployment, I was hired by an organization that seemed to hold promise for career growth and development. After I was stable in my position, Doug made his first exit, which left me devastated. Although it was heartbreaking and I felt empty, Doug and I had truly endured ridiculously traumatic experiences. In addition to my surgery and downsizing, I would be remiss to omit the most difficult challenge of all: my ex-husband John's legal challenges. While seeking employment, I took a course towards obtaining my doctorate degree. I wanted to start slowly, so I registered for one class over the summer. I was interested to see how I would adjust to academic life after being out of school for so many years. After class one evening, I entered my car, picked up my mobile phone, and noticed several missed calls from Doug. I returned the call and the conversation went something like this:

"Hey, sweetie. Everything okay? I noticed you've been calling."

"Hey, baby. The FBI called me trying to get in touch with you," he replied.

"Really? I'm not surprised they want to talk to me, considering who I was married to, but I haven't done anything wrong. And why would they call you?"

"I guess just to get in touch with you. He left me a number. Take it down, call him, then call me back." I agreed, then proceeded to hang up and call the agent.

Doug and I were referring to a news story in which my ex-husband John was listed as being under investigation for misappropriation of funds. As I called the agent, I couldn't help but be a bit nervous. I never had to deal with any type of legal issue. To gain clarity, I called my divorce attorney to let her know I'd been contacted. She and her legal colleague assured me that it was okay to move forward with the questioning because it was very clear I hadn't done anything wrong. I had always kept my personal bank accounts separate from John's. I had my own career long before he came into the picture. In addition, we had been separated and divorced almost two years at that point, so I was just as surprised as the public. Ultimately, John settled with the court and was sentenced. This was a very stressful, painful time for everyone connected to John. However, I believe my son, who was only twelve years old at the time, was affected the most. He wasn't old enough to fully process that a man whom he had looked up to, now faced criminal charges.

In addition, the media storm that followed was horrific. I was fortunate to keep my then two-year-old daughter sheltered, but I wasn't so successful with my son. The worst experience of it all was when the newspaper published the names of my children; I could not believe it. As one who holds a degree in Journalism myself, I always thought publishing the names of underage children unethical. To make matters worse, Christopher wasn't John's biological son. John was pretty much estranged from Christopher at that point, by his own choice. They also published Doug's name in relation to the story. It seemed like the local paper and news stations reported daily on the story. While I believe in the freedom of the press, I also believe the press should be sensitive to certain stories where children are concerned. In addition, of all the pictures and video they must have had on my ex-husband, I don't understand why they insisted on using the same picture and video from his swearing in ceremony. Those pictures included me and we were clearly divorced.

It was truly a traumatic experience for all of us. I'm surprised Doug lasted as long as he did that first go-round. However, timing was the problem. I was just starting to get back on my feet financially when the first breakup came and caught me off guard. Being with him filled a vacant spot that I wanted filled and, at the time, needed in my life. However, that "vacant spot" was the place that should have been filled by God and my own love of self. Over the course of the relationship, which lasted four and a half years, he and I broke up whenever his uncertainty or my insecurity got the best of us. I always took him back. During our "breaks," I appeared to be hard as a rock. Of course, over time, Doug showed up on the phone and at my door, apologizing. Of course, I made him sweat for a few weeks, but I always took him back, as I'm sure he knew I would.

In January of 2015, I warned him that it would be the absolute last time I could take him back. He promised that he loved me and was in love with me. He said he was sure he wanted to marry me, but I was tired of his instability and indecision. At some point, I knew we were either going to get married, or I needed to step away. I simply couldn't waste time any longer. It had already been four years. He assured me that I could trust him. He knew he wanted to be with me and my children. I was hurting with him and hurting without him. I wanted to believe him, even though my heart told me different. Maya Angelou said, "When people show you who they are, believe them the first time." I embraced it, repeated it, and taught it to others. However, when it was my turn to put that wisdom into action, I couldn't do it. It's obvious how broken I was at the time. Only a broken person could give a person chance after chance and hope the ending would be different. The most popular definition of insanity in action is doing the same thing over and over and expecting a different result. I wasn't insane. However, because I hadn't yet done the work to empower myself and tap back into my own strength, I was weak. One of our friends joked a couple of years earlier that my relationship with Doug was like me riding on a hamster wheel–moving and doing all the work, but not going anywhere. At the time, I laughed, but she turned out to be exactly right.

By August, I'd grown tired of Doug's excuses and hesitations on marriage. A loved one suggested that I cut him off and move on with my life. I agreed that I needed to release him, but I wasn't sure I had the strength to do it without conversation. If I had a conversation with Doug, he would've talked me into remaining in the relationship because he knew I was vulnerable. Furthermore, he knew I loved him. I allowed his instability and indecision to feed my insecurities and, over the course of almost five years, I became so emotionally weak that it was amazing I could stand on my own at all. I loved him, and I desperately wanted to save the relationship. The problem was that I didn't love myself enough. In fact, I think I loved him more than I loved myself, which is dangerous. When I accepted that reality, I knew I had to cut him off abruptly and immediately.

Later that night when he called, I let the phone ring. The next morning, I let the phone ring. He left message after message, voicemail after voicemail. Nevertheless, I was not going to answer the phone. As one might imagine, that one action sent Doug into a frenzy. He called multiple times a day as his anxiety grew. In my mind, he didn't deserve my presence or even the luxury of hearing my voice. I felt as though I had been bamboozled and he had strung me along. He had come to me in January requesting yet another chance. He assured me that he was sincere and ready. He even told me he would have a ring by June, if only I would be patient. But it was now August, and his words still didn't line up with his actions. I had to release him abruptly because I had a weakness for Doug and he knew it.

After a week, Doug continued to call and I finally picked

up the phone. We decided to meet at a restaurant to chat about what needed to happen with our future. At that point, we were obviously nervous. We talked and cried publicly, and finally decided to give each other some space. Well, that only lasted about three weeks. Doug showed up at my door, confessing that he had made up his mind that he wanted us to get married. I wanted to believe him, but my intuition was speaking loud and clear that it was time to end the relationship. On several occasions, I told Annette that God's Spirit had been telling me to let him go. Everything inside of me was screaming it. She encouraged me to be strong and release him if that was what God was leading me to do. She also told me that once I was obedient, if Doug was meant to be in my world, he would return. I knew in my heart I was supposed to let him go, but I simply did not have the courage. Well, just as Mother Maya Angelou taught Oprah Winfrey, and Oprah Winfrey taught the world, "God whispers before He yells." For over a year, God whispered to my heart to let him go. I just didn't want to obey, nor did I think I could obey.

Well, I didn't, and there was a heavy price to pay. In September of 2015, after we had reconciled once more,

Doug asked me to go to the jewelry store to search for my engagement ring. He had already picked one that he liked, but he wanted to know what I liked. While I was at work, he emailed a few pictures from a website and, ironically, I chose the same engagement ring he had picked out for me. It wasn't oversized or gaudy, but it reflected my style at the time: simple and elegant. On the following Sunday at the jewelry store, I tried on the ring. We even chose his wedding band. We had a great time as his friend held his camera phone and shared our joy. We even posed together, with both our hands aligned atop one another, sporting our future nuptial bling. Little did I know that by the end of October, not only would the rings no longer be in the equation, but Doug and I wouldn't even be in a relationship. Doug's fears of commitment rose yet again. In response to what he called pressure, he decided he wasn't ready and wanted to end the relationship. Interestingly, he was the one who said he was ready, after I was prepared to walk away, but then he flipped and decided to call it "pressure."

Our final breakup was October 17, 2015. I was devastated. Thoughts raced through my mind as I questioned how in the world I allowed myself to get caught up with Doug yet again, only to be let down again. It was a ridiculous cycle that needed to end. I only remember the specific day because I had a mini-marathon (13K) the next day. How could he ask for me to come back a fourth time, only to let me down again? I trusted him. I believed in him. And, for what?

Taking a deeper look, I realized that it was my own self-betrayal that led to my demise emotionally. I heard God speaking but I chose to believe in a man who had shown me who he was over and over again. Mother Maya Angelou and Oprah Winfrey had warned. God himself had spoken very loudly, very clearly that I needed to leave that relationship, but I didn't. My own disobedience broke my heart, not Doug.

Things got worse as I continued to toggle between playing the victim and owning my responsibility. A few weeks later, Doug finally told me that he had reconnected with an ex-girlfriend from his younger days. He hadn't seen the woman in almost thirty years. I called him in an anxious moment, still heartbroken and somewhat in shock. I knew in my heart already, even though he had lied on multiple occasions, but I thought I would ask once more: "Is there someone else?" He answered with a sigh and told me the truth. The fear-based anger rushed through my system, but I calmly told him I would drop his items off at his house.

Once I arrived, we talked and somewhat mutually agreed that it was over. Then, I lost it. My hurt and anger consumed me as I swung, beating Doug in the chest as tears streamed down my cheeks. "How could you do this to me? How could you do this to us? And what about my kids? You begged me to come back to you, then you turn around and do this?" Doug grabbed my arms in shock and disbelief. He held me to the floor, encouraging me to 'get ahold of myself.' He'd turned my life upside down in a matter of weeks, and now he wanted me to get ahold of myself? I had let him go, but he wanted to get back in and look for rings. I felt played, hoodwinked, bamboozled. I lost it. But my response is the typical response of a woman who has lost herself and given too much of herself away to an unworthy cause. Had I loved myself enough, if I were living in a whole place spiritually, I not only would have obeyed my intuition, I also wouldn't have allowed Doug to have that place in my heart that only belonged to God. Nothing should ever come before God. Take this as a warning. Anything placed before Him will inevitably fail. After my outburst, Doug and I eventually hugged and parted ways. I sped home, went to my laptop, and deleted every picture of Doug and I on Facebook. Then, I blocked him. To this very day, even though I have forgiven him and we are friendly with one another, I still have him blocked.

To be transparent, before I blocked him, I stepped on the "crazy" side and did something I have never done and prayerfully will never go so low to do again. My actions were the result of a depleted woman who gave too much of herself away. It happens all the time to other people, but never had it happened to me. In fact, in the past I snobbishly snubbed women who sank to such petty behavior. Some women cut tires, scratch cars, break windows, do all kinds of crazy stuff. Well, me and my ego did something just as silly. I still can't believe what I did. I went to his Facebook page and intuitively recognized his "flame." Believe it or not, he and I were that connected; intuition is real and I was right. In my weak, insecure, fearful state of mind, I sent her a collage of pictures of me, Doug and our intertwined families via inbox. In my emotionally mentally cluttered daze, I wanted her to know that she wasn't stepping between a fling, we were family and there were children involved. Not only that, she needed to know, that we were beautiful, and we were beautiful together. Yes, that was my 'crazy,' shameful moment. As if I thought that contacting her would make a difference, like most women, I'm sure she didn't care. It's hilariously embarrassing to me now, but it's the truth. It still amazes me how intuitively connected I was to Doug that I recognized her by intuition, I'm sure it scared the heck out of him. Looking back, I think it was more of God speaking loudly to me that that relationship needed to be over. After that, I pretended not to know her name to everyone, except my best friend.

I now realize that Doug was a soul mate. Not the kind you marry, but the kind that serves your life as a mirror to help you grow. Once you learn the life lessons they have taught, the relationship must end and life must move forward.

By the time the holidays approached a couple of months later, I received phone calls confirming that Doug's "new friend" would be coming to town. Two months before,

Doug had put a ring on my finger and asked me to marry him. Now, he was bringing a different woman to town? I was in emotional shock. I fell into a major depression. What in the world was wrong with him? Better yet, what in the world was wrong with me? My heart sank. I felt like I was going to die. That was truly the lowest point in my life. To make matters worse, he was planning to entertain her at Ricky and Annette's new home. They planned a major housewarming and New Year's Eve party. I couldn't believe any of it. Ricky wanted Doug at the party, and Annette wanted me there; it was hard for all of us.

Once I heard his new interest was coming to town, I thought I would call him to try to talk some sense into him. Anytime he and I broke up prior to this, he was always respectful. I'd never heard of him dating, or even talking to, another girl. This time, he was acting out in a big way. I just knew I could get him to do the right thing, so I phoned him. That conversation went from expressing my hurt and asking him not to bring her to the party, to him replying, "I can't promise you that, Lisa."

I responded, "So you don't care about me and the

kids anymore? You just begged me to come back to you in January and put a ring on my finger two months ago in October. Now, you just don't care?" My frustration transformed into anger as my words became decorated with yelling and profanity. The call eventually ended with me bluffing a subtle threat, which left him thinking twice. But that subtle threat was no more than idle chatter pouring from my emotionally bruised heart. I later told my friend "Shelly" about the conversation. She said, "Oh, and what you gon' hurt him with, a Bible?" We laughed hysterically.

The amazing thing is that God is so faithful and understanding that, in all of this, He had already planned 'a way of escape' for me. As it turned out, my younger brother and his family (who live in Houston, Texas) planned a New Year's Eve stay in the mountains of North Carolina in a cabin not far from Asheville. As I poured my heart out to my sister-in-law "Kendall," she immediately told me to pack up the kids and head to the mountains to spend the holidays with them. Thankfully, I had the money for the last-minute trip, and we jumped on the road two days later.

As 2016 rolled in and everyone else celebrated, I wiped

droves of tears from my eyes whenever no one was looking. At one point, I ran to the bedroom just to release and cry out loud. That was the most excruciating, overwhelming pain I ever experienced. In addition, it was embarrassing that Doug would bring "some girl" around our mutual friends, my circle, just two months after we broke up. It was crazy. It was unbelievable. Quite frankly, it was worse than my worst nightmare. Most of the people at the party hadn't even heard that we were no longer together. From what I heard, several people asked, "Where is Lisa, and who in the hell is that with Doug?" Learning the sentiment of onlookers brought immediate comfort to my heart, but that was only the beginning.

PART TWO

The BounceBack

After leaving Asheville, the kids and I drove down to the Chapel Hill and Oxford, North Carolina, to visit my "Aunt Bonnie" and "Uncle George." As a pastor, Uncle George offered me encouraging words and prayed that God would heal my heart. He also advised me to pray for Doug. He told me that one day Doug would call, and when he did, I should greet him as a Christian, forgive him and pray for him. I was broken. I couldn't imagine him ever calling or me ever praying for him. I knew at some point, I would forgive him because I love God and forgiveness is a basic principle of Christianity. While I was at their home, a pivotal moment occurred that led to the next step in my healing process.

On the morning of January 2, 2016 while having coffee alone in the kitchen, I scrolled Facebook and read a post from Life Coach Angel Richards. It was titled "3 Lessons I learned in 2015." I immediately found myself listening to her SoundCloud message. I knew that God had me in that very moment for a reason. My heart was aching, but she opened that message with her truth about her divorce from her husband and friend. It resonated with my heart and pierced my very spirit. In her first lesson, she shared the reality that we need to 'get over things, and get over them quickly.' I didn't know how to get over it. I didn't even know how to start, but she was right. If I wallowed too long, my children would suffer and that price was way too heavy to pay. I had to move forward. She talked about several of her personal experiences and gave tools that, not only led to her continuing to thrive, but offered me a line of safety, as well. I found it to be truly amazing that she could be so authentic. I listened to her speak and drew correlations to my own challenge in order to survive my season of heartbreak. I wasn't sure how I was going to move forward, but listening to Angel provided hope. I held onto her every word. I'd heard about Angel months prior, and even began her 21 Day Challenge, but I never completed it. Every time I listened to a portion of it, then spent time with my then boyfriend, I felt a tug in my spirit because my actions were contradictory to her messages.

After I returned to Ohio, I listened to every free message Angel had on SoundCloud. When I wasn't listening to her, I listened to T.D. Jakes or Joel Osteen daily on YouTube. My cell phone bill was ridiculously high from January to March, but it was worth every cent. I needed to heal, and I was finally on my way. Doug was like a drug to me. The withdrawals after he was gone were so severe that I could barely function. I thought I was going to die. The hurt was only amplified by the fact that we shared the same friendship circle, as our best friends were married to each other. During those times, Annette would call me and I'd quickly make up an excuse to hang up the phone. Talking to her was a constant reminder of Doug. I couldn't remember him and heal at the same time. Most calls, she didn't even mention his name unless I asked, we were besties. So many of our conversations over the years centered around our relationships, kids, careers, church and goals. The mere mention of her husband's name made me think of Doug. The only way I knew to survive and save myself was to cut off every reminder, which meant limiting our phone conversations. I hoped she would understand because I was emotionally drowning, and I had to get to shore.

For years, Annette and I talked multiple times a day. My new behavior was very hurtful to her. While I apologized, it's taken a long time for our friendship to get back on track. In some ways, it may never be the same. That was something that she and I both admitted to one another. We were 'sisters' and, although we love one another, there was a breach on both sides. I was hurt when she allowed Doug to bring his 'date' to the New Year's Eve party in her home, less than two months after we broke up. Although I tried to be understanding, he was her husband's best friend, after all. Hadn't she told me a million times that I needed to set Doug free so he could work on his own issues and, at the same time, give myself some healing space so that my confidence could be restored? Yes, but I was so broken and hollow inside. I didn't have the courage to take the first step, and I ignored my own intuition.

I also had an unexpected breach in a friendship that I thought was a solid escape from what had become "Doug's circle of friends." That was with my sister-in-law "Theresa" who was also my sorority sister. She and I went through a lot of transition together, including when she was dating her ex-husband "Randy," marriage, our mutual pregnancies, bed rest, and finally, both of our divorces. Our sisterhood formed organically. I believe that was divinely connected so we could support one another, when needed. We were there for one another throughout several major life experiences. However, our friendship was tested not long after my final devastating breakup with Doug.

Three weeks after the breakup in October I went with Theresa to Memphis for a getaway with a group of her friends. It was a great idea in theory, and it was exactly what I needed to begin moving forward. However, in my mind, I continued to rehearse the breakup with Doug. Even worse, I had learned the week prior that he'd reconnected with a woman from his past. On the way, I called my favorite aunt, Dorothy. She was eighty-five years old and sassy as ever. Her husband, my Uncle Dicky, answered the phone. He told me she was still sleeping. They were up a little late, hosting a couple of other relatives over Thanksgiving dinner. I asked him to tell her that I called and that I was on the road, but would call her later that evening. Unfortunately, I was caught up in my own world, so I didn't call that evening.

The group of us experienced Memphis that weekend. Although I was with a fun group of people, I'm sure my pain, anger and "victim" chatter, which sometimes spewed from my mouth, put a damper on the festivities. At one point, the one who appeared to be the oldest of the crew, "Renee" said, "Look, everybody on this trip has something going on. But, when we travel, we leave it at home and focus on having a good time. Everything else can wait. Now we are going to party and I'm going to give you this shot of Fireball to make sure you enjoy yourself." Once she said that, I let my guard down, agreed, and took that shot like a pro. Renee gave me a very timely reminder when I desperately needed it. Granted, I was living in a broken space at the time, but she reminded me not to let my issues cripple me.

Furthermore, it wasn't worth letting Doug steal any more of my joy. I didn't grow up with a silver spoon in my mouth, so resilience was a way of life. Even though I'd given a great part of myself away to him, and landed at rock bottom, I was sure I could get through the disappointment. I needed to toughen up and get it together. She will probably never know, but I appreciate Renee so much for that.

As the weekend continued, I did my best to suppress the pain, with or without a drink. I enjoyed the rest of the weekend. We visited The Lorraine Motel (now a museum), where Dr. Martin Luther King, Jr. was assassinated, as well as another museum across the street, where James Earl Ray hatefully committed the crime. We laughed and talked about future outings, most notably, Theresa's upcoming birthday in February. She wanted to plan an excursion to Florida and we were all in. Then, on that Sunday morning, the big blow came.

I learned that I had lost my Aunt Dorothy. At 4:30 a.m. Memphis time, my phone rang. It was my mother. My Aunt Dorothy had a heart attack at home and paramedics were unable to resuscitate her. This was extremely painful. I let out a loud gasp, awakening the other ladies from their slumber. Honestly, my mind could not grasp that my Aunt Dorothy was gone. I'd just tried to call her a couple of days prior. My procrastination caused me to miss out on an opportunity to have one last conversation with the eldest woman in my family. Oh, how I miss our talks! I made other important calls to family and eventually started packing since we planned to return to Ohio later that day. I'm sure the other ladies didn't know what to think. I had known Theresa for years, but I didn't know the other ladies well at all.

After returning home and getting back to my normal routine, Theresa made plans for her birthday trip to Florida in February. It was going to be especially cool for me since I'd get to see a guy from college. He would often call to check on me or pray with me when I was depressed. It was January and Theresa's birthday was a few weeks away. Imagine my surprise when, one afternoon, Theresa called to tell me that I was no longer welcome on the trip. She said she'd noticed by my conversation that I was still depressed when, at one point, she thought I was further along in my healing process. From that point on, she thought it was best that she keep her friends separate, meaning she would hang out with me separately from her other friends. I was almost in shock because we had both, over the course of time, introduced one another to our mutual circles. I even invited her into my Sister Circle. I also took off work to go with her to court during her divorce and custody battle.

I was nothing but supportive of her, just as she had been supportive of me. However, she now preferred to do things differently, so I accepted it and adjusted, although I was deeply hurt.

After that conversation, I pulled away. We didn't talk much at all, except for the few times she called me. I always answered her questions and responded to whatever she said, but I kept things very brief due to my own pain and lack of trust. After several months of cold distance, she called, told me she missed me and I told her we needed to talk, I missed her too. When we sat down, I told her how I felt and she apologized for being selfish. She admitted that she was just tired of my constant back and forth with Doug. Quite frankly, she didn't want to hear it anymore. I had worn her out. While I understood her sentiment, we were much too close for her not to be transparent in how she truly felt. Had she told me up front that she was exhausted from hearing about my on-and-off relationship I would have put things into perspective and understood. She was exhausted from the tears I shed. She was tired of hearing me go on and on about it, only for me to take him back.

From a spiritual perspective, the deterioration of my friendship with Theresa and the fact that I'd pulled away from others is indicative of pruning. Sometimes God allows things and people to be removed for a season so that something more beautiful can emerge. God was teaching me to be my own best friend and to stand on my own again. It was too hard to communicate with my mutual friends I shared with Doug, then the issue with Theresa emerged and I was pretty much on my own. It was a part of the healing process and God allowed it and now I truly understand it was all for my good.

After we talked we gained mutual understanding, after all, she had never told me how she felt until then and I can't read minds. Communication is key. If thoughts aren't translated into words nothing good results. Because of a lack of communication, we almost lost our friendship. I felt betrayed. I had been there for her as she was for me. I've learned since, in my own healing process, that when loved ones are presented with situations like ours, communication is vital. Not only that, but those involved should accept one another where they are in life, and love them in and through that space. Over the course of time, things always change and hopefully, get better. I loved Theresa like a sister and thankfully, we got through that challenge. Everything is forgiven. Only time will tell as our friendship continues to heal and grow. I know now that God designed it that way so that I would learn to lean on Him and trust in Him.

Overall, the stress of the relationship between Doug and me caused tension amongst the whole group of friends. I'm confident that everyone was happy to see that relationship end. God allowed it for a reason, which I now understand was for me to find myself. For that, I will forever be grateful. In my pain and insecurity, I became co-dependent. Prior to being broken, that was never my personality. I was always "there" for everyone else. At that point, though, I needed myself. I've learned the hard way that, no matter how loyal, dedicated and forgiving an individual may be, he or she simply cannot allow themselves to be taken for granted. That type of love is toxic for the soul. It can only end in absolute misery and brokenness unless there is real change–the kind that only God can impose. It doesn't happen over the course of a few months, as I had so many times wanted to believe.

It took a lot of self-work and time alone for me to finally heal. In addition to a life coach, I was introduced to the Emotional Polarity Technique (EPT). This amazing healing tool was key to me rediscovering the woman I am. For at least two years prior, I had heard about this enzyme specialist named Chanelle, who also assisted with individuals' emotional healing to help them move forward from their past pain and issues. Several of my friends and associates saw her, but I wasn't too keen on holistic care necessarily. The fact that insurance didn't cover any type of naturopathic care didn't help. However, in February of 2016, when I was in the throes of despair, I was willing to try anything to heal my aching heart. EPT was different for me because it uses muscle testing, which is something I never experienced. Muscle testing is supposed to isolate issues. Then, through EPT forgiveness exercises, one will release whatever hindrances are discovered. I often refer to EPT as years of therapy in one hour. I've done traditional therapy on more than one occasion and although I had very effective therapists, with amazing results, EPT moved me forward quicker and the areas healed were much deeper.

Chanelle is a God-send and has truly been a blessing to

my life. During our first session, she looked at me and said, "God did not create you to be small." I broke down crying because it was in that moment that I remembered who God created me to be. I was that beautiful young lady with goals and dreams of being a professional vocalist and actress. I was still that young lady whom I had left in New York so many years prior. In that moment, I shared my personal story with Chanelle, which included my experiences in the entertainment industry and my goals of authoring my own books. God used her to help me find myself and my creativity again.

As time went on, I continued to work on myself. Over the course of several months, I longed to hear from Doug, even if only to receive an apology. Well, almost a year to the date of the heartbreak, I received a text. It was a surprise but, at that point, I neither needed nor wanted an apology. I'm sure God allowed me to receive that contact in that moment for that very reason. I'd forgiven him and set him free; a conversation was no longer necessary. It's funny how things work out. He asked if we could talk and initially I didn't respond for a couple of days. Eventually, we connected and all my questions were answered. What

I learned in the conversation was, quite frankly, great for my ego. It was nice to finally get closure. It felt great to be strong enough to not be "moved" by a man who, at one time, made my heart flutter and my toes curl just by being in his presence. Nevertheless, it was clear that I couldn't allow him back into my life. We could be friendly but, most likely, we would never be real friends again.

Actions have consequences. Doug had lost a "ready-made" family, who loved him unconditionally. He lost my level of love that would have supported him forever. As for me, the consequences of continually taking him back and ignoring my intuition was weakened self-esteem and several disappointments that ultimately ended with me being at the lowest point of my life. There was also a mutual loss of respect, although neither of us would ever admit it. The only reason I loved Doug so hard, and tolerated his indecision, was because I didn't love myself enough. Again, I was seeking to fill the void of my own identity in that space that I released on the drive home from New York. Deep down inside, I thought I could fix Doug. I looked at him and I saw the great man he could be, the man he had the potential to be—not the man that was standing before me. Like many women, I fell in love with potential, which amounts to an illusion. I created the illusion in my mind based upon secrets that we shared during our many nights of pillow talk. He's not a bad person. He's a good person with a good heart. He possesses that unique quality of speaking to a woman with such attentiveness that she feels as though she's the only woman in the world. He's humanly flawed like the rest of us. Perfection in relationships doesn't exist. But, if we remain open, God will send us the perfect, imperfect mate.

Despite all the hurt and pain, I have absolutely no regrets because it took that low point for me to look at myself and find that girl who lost herself along the way. My road to re-discovery began with the realization that the healing had to begin and end with me. I was the one holding onto the toxicity, even though everything inside of me screamed for me to let go. I was the one playing with fire. I was the one who didn't have the courage to walk away. That last go-round of our relationship was the one we all thought would stick, especially since we had already picked out the ring. But, God had other plans. I needed to get back on track with God's plan so I could complete His will for my life. Chanelle was right: God did not create me to be small. He never intended for me step away from the path I was on in New York. I made an emotional decision without consulting with God first. For twelve years, I lived outside of myself. I moved with the ebbs and flows of life, without true intention. Most of my life, I had lived fully intuitively and in touch with my spirit. However, once I stepped outside of God's will, and lost myself inside of a life of "normalcy," I couldn't truly hear God's spirit. Even when I did, I didn't take heed in most cases.

In the following months, I continued to heal and eventually bounced back. Friends encouraged me when they could, but I had to do the tough work myself. I had to learn to love myself all over again. Ultimately, there is no one to blame, but myself. That's not to excuse anyone's hurtful actions; however, I would have never been in the situation if I hadn't betrayed myself. I wouldn't have been in this place if I'd have stayed within my passion and purpose. Who knows what amazing things God had in store for me in New York? I had connections. I had a marketable 'look' and I was getting noticed.

However, I live life with no regrets. Given the same situation, I still would have chosen Christopher over anything the world has to offer. If I were given a second chance, when I returned to Ohio, I would not have been so anxious to get married to John, so much so that I ignored the signs God sent me. It also wasn't beneficial for me to ignore the constant messages God sent me regarding my relationship with Doug. In both cases, there was a price to pay that left me lost and depressed. Listening to intuition is key to living a passionate life; it's an inside job that exudes on the outside. I could have saved myself a lot of heartache in my marriage to John, and in the relationship with Doug, had I listened and been obedient at the appropriate time. I loved both men. They were both friends that somehow grew into something that I never predicted. However, the seasons for both of those relationships are over. I now share the lessons to help other women avoid similar mistakes. When entering times of transition, be still, pray, fast, and listen. You might just be surprised at what God says to you. Be obedient and pay attention to the signs that confirm and guide. While it will require faith to step into the unknown, when you are living your own truth that comes from inside your own spirit, you will not only be fulfilled--you'll live and walk in God's perfect will for your life.

PART THREE

From Heartbreak to Wholeness

My journey to recovery was a series of emotional ups and downs over the course of a year. Some might find it interesting that I use the term "recovery"; however, toxic love can be an addiction. The road to healing was a hard one, but I am truly grateful for it all. It was on that road that I regained my identity. I am now thankful that God allowed me to meet and love both my ex-husband John and my ex-boyfriend, Doug. I am also thankful that God took the relationship with Doug away after I continued to ignore His voice telling me to let it go. Most of all, I'm grateful for the biggest lesson and takeaway: to love myself first. Both John and Doug taught me how to love myself first by not loving me the way I needed to be loved; they could only love me in their own love languages. Although they both said they loved me, their actions were never consistent with what I had in mind, because my love language was different. Out of the many relationships I've had in my forty plus years of life, these two men taught me the important lesson of loving myself first.

Although I didn't realize it at the time, I healed and moved forward by doing things that were comforting to my heart from moment to moment. I only hoped they would make my pain go away. Eventually, as time went on, my heart healed. After almost a year, my heart had healed and I didn't feel any bitterness. I only felt love. If I wanted to have a healthy relationship, I needed to work on myself. In addition, I felt, and still feel, God pulling on my heart to educate other women to remain true to themselves and the importance of holding onto themselves as they navigate through life. I truly feel that it is a charge from God. It is my responsibility to "pay it forward" and help someone else through their pain. If possible, I want to even help them avoid it.

One of my mentors, author and publisher, Valerie L. Coleman, mentioned it might be helpful to not only tell my story in a memoir, but also to summarize my journey in a series of easy-to-follow steps about how to move forward without bitterness. I participated in her memoir project and summarized the steps into this book, The BounceBack: From Heartbreak to Wholeness. The steps might remind you of what AA calls the 12-Step Program; however, although The BounceBack details the series of nine steps that I took, they were not necessarily in this full order. I was so broken that I literally moved between them, depending on what felt good from moment to moment, day to day. Eventually, that led to my freedom beyond the pain. It took a lot of work and self-examination to love myself again, but it led to my soul's restoration.

If you are hurting, depressed, devoid of individuality because you've given too much of yourself away, or you feel lost, continue reading. The following pages contain wisdom earned and learned through my pain. Not only will this wisdom potentially prevent you from becoming lost, but it will also help lead you to wholeness if you are trying to find your way back. The BounceBack: From Heartbreak to Wholeness is designed to 'jumpstart' your journey to self-realization and authentic identification. You can begin again from a place of power. You can complete every dream and goal that God has put into your heart.

Step 1: Prayed for Restoration and Guidance. Although praying may sound cliché, I have always believed in God and His redemptive power offered through His Son, Jesus. Therefore, I knew I would eventually heal and come back together. However, in the depths of my despair and depression, I felt so low that sometimes, I felt like I would die. My heart was truly broken, and I needed it to be healed. I now realize that it wasn't so much the end of my relationship with John that caused my heart to ache so badly; it was amplified pain that resulted from my own self-abandonment. I forgot who I was. I let go of my passion, my goals. I lost who I was as an individual; hitting rock bottom was merely the impact of my own mistakes. I was so busy taking care of everyone else that I forgot to take care of myself.

During my marriage to John, I got lost. Instead of spending some time alone to restore myself after the divorce, I entered the relationship with Doug after only a year of being unmarried. The danger of entering a relationship without being fully restored to self is that you tend to take on the lifestyle and purpose of whomever you are attached to. Unfortunately, when that relationship ends, you could possibly feel devastated and void because you took on your partner's identity. Who are you without that partner? In fact, the hollow feeling often replaces what you might have thought was love. It could have been false fulfillment because the emotions didn't originate from a healthy, whole space. God never intended for any human to be fulfilled by another human. No human completes another human. Fulfillment and completion can only come from God. Therefore, we must seek Him for restoration and guidance. In my journey, the pain of divorce was compounded with another pain. In the end, it felt like two divorces. That type of low, deep depression can only be healed by prayer, good counsel and if necessary, medication. Hope rests in God. I knew if I was ever going to live empowered again, I had to seek Him continually and allow Him to do whatever work in me He deemed necessary.

Step 2: Forgave Myself. One of the most difficult things

I have ever had to do was look beyond the hurtful actions of my exes and truly look at myself. I was the cause of a lot of my pain. This is not to forego or disregard anyone else's careless behavior. I just know now that if I had truly loved myself enough to hold on to myself, I never would have been in either situation. More specifically, I would have never allowed anyone to be irresponsible with the love I gave. I also am now aware that people have their own issues. If they are not healed or whole, or they don't recognize they need self-work, there is no way they can be who or what I need them to be. The reality which I was seeking was inside of me already. I just needed to recognize and embrace it--self-love.

Ultimately, I forgave myself for abandoning myself on the drive back from New York to Dayton. I also forgave myself for staying in unhealthy relationships. I forgave myself for the time I wasted living a life that didn't align with what was in my heart. I've been a creative my whole life, whether it's been singing or writing. Throughout the years that I spent living outside of myself, I talked about writing, even started new projects. But I never completed a full work. Singing wasn't even in the equation. I forgave myself for being naïve, and for the resulting depression that had a severe impact on other areas of my life. When I was broken, I could barely get out of bed in the morning. I went to work daily, but I wasn't fully focused on the tasks at hand. Therefore, I knew I had to make some changes. One key move was when I stepped away from an executive board position in a community service organization. I loved the organization and the people it served, however, I needed to focus on myself and my children. I knew I had to save myself before I could help anyone else. I had to get my household in order. I forgave myself for any and every mistake I made as well as the residual pain it left.

Step 3: Forgave Others. I used to brag about how I forgave everyone. Lack of forgiveness wasn't an issue for me, I touted. Well, God was listening because I was tested in that very area, in big ways. I had to forgive both John and Doug for loving me in their own love languages. They're human, they didn't have the capacity to fill my empty void. It was my job to love myself and allow God to fill the void. I've learned that an individual's ability to love is based on their own capacity to do so. It is often based upon their own life experiences and the foundations on which it is built. People show and interpret love differently, that's why it is so important to be 'equally yoked' with the individuals with whom we enter relationships. Neither of them could love me in the way in which I needed to be loved because we love and showed love differently. In addition, there were other issues and areas in which we differed, such as how we viewed commitment, finances, friendships, etc. People, in general, can be innately selfish; but hopefully at some point we realize it and learn better ways to be more considerate. I had to forgive Doug and John individually.

John, having been my husband, was held on a higher plane of responsibility. One would think he would have been the man with which I could be transparent; however, relationships and marriages should be invested in to bring out the best in each partner. Perhaps our differences made it impossible for the both of us. When a partner insists on loving the other from his or her own perspective, and they're not willing to give the other partner what they need, there is no way that couple will make it. I forgave him for the alleged rumors. People approached me during the divorce process, stating things that he 'supposedly' said, even some stating that he accused me of having an affair. I forgave him and the people who brought me the information, because it wasn't true and it didn't matter. I also had to forgive him for the supposed rumors that placed blame upon me for his legal issues; he and I both knew that I had nothing to do with any of it. The reality is we married when I was thirty-five years old, long after I had been secure in my own career. Not only did I make more money than him, but I had been raised to keep my own separate bank account for my security as a woman. It was okay to have a shared account, but I was taught to always hold my own as well, and I did. God knew better, and so did John, but the community rumor mill had no idea. I knew that I had nothing to do with the things of which he had been accused. Furthermore, I have never cheated on anyone in my life. I forgave him for all the arguments, the points of intimidation, and for any dishonesty, whether it existed or not. I had to forgive him. I needed peace. I only pray now that John has found it in his heart to forgive me for ways that I may have offended and hurt him. I pray this for his own peace of mind.

I also had to forgive Doug, which was much more difficult than forgiving John, for several reasons. First, by the time my relationship with Doug ended, I had already been divorced five years. Doug had entered my life when I was at a low point. I initially met him while I was separated and going through a divorce. We shared a friendship that we build over the course of a year, before we began a committed dating relationship. However, I was still vulnerable. I hadn't fully restored my life; I hadn't bounced back. Doug gave me what I needed at the time, for a season, which was love and affection based upon pure friendship. My relationship with Doug also provided the desired connection in a relationship that I craved. Unfortunately, it was temporary; it could not be sustained. Even after choosing a ring, Doug betrayed everything we had built, friendship included. It wasn't the break up, it was his careless actions immediately after the split. Looking back, I know that too, was God-ordained. Due to my intuitive nature, I could feel and predict when our relationship was headed for the rocks, even for the last time.

One might wonder, if I was so intuitive, why did I allow him to enter and exit my life like he did in the first place? I heard my spirit speaking, very loudly in fact, screaming for me to release him. But, I wanted what I wanted. I wanted to believe the words he said to me. I wanted to believe that we would surprise everyone and make it even though, deep down in my heart, I already knew the answer. I knew deep down we were not going to make it as a couple, and ultimately, his actions finally confirmed it.

I wanted to believe we would have the love that I felt early in the relationship, but God did not allow it. Over time, I came to accept it. To the critics and some of those who loved me, they felt like Doug knew I was vulnerable and played on my weaknesses. They said that 'to him, I was easy prey.' Honestly, I can't say that I believe that he entered our relationship with ill will at all. In fact, he not only told me he was ready to move forward, he told some his friends that were in our circle. While it is true that I was not whole or loving myself enough, I won't 'criminalize' him; I will say that at the time, he had his own self-work to do. For him to continually build me up, let me down, and then come back with promises of our future together was reckless disregard and downright selfish. However, I had to own that I allowed it because I was broken. Iyanla Vanzant teaches audiences to "calling a thing a thing," and that's exactly what I had to do so I could heal.

Having done my self-work, it's possible that Doug and I never would have had a relationship at all if I was operating from a fully whole state of self. For four and a half years I rode an emotional roller coaster, but I rode willingly because I was empty. Now that I've had that experience, my heart truly goes out to other women who consistently move in and out of relationships with the same man. The inconsistency may not be for the same reasons as ours, but there is nothing healthy about anyone remaining in a yo-yo marriage or relationship, yet it happens all the time.

I forgave Doug with my words long before I believed them. I said the words from my mouth long before my heart felt them. I knew that if I was ever going to be free, I had to forgive him. Forgiveness is a key foundation of Christianity. I wanted to move on without baggage, without the weight of my pain, without the residue. When everything first happened, he didn't appear to be sorry, which made it more difficult. He just seemed to keep on stepping. When he finally reached out almost a year later, I learned that things weren't as simple as they seemed.

When we sat down to chat, not only did he answer all

my questions, but he was honest about the impact of the relationship on his life. We both talked about the lessons we learned. I was a life teacher for him, and he was a life teacher for me. It's amazing how God gave me closure to that relationship when I no longer needed it. For months, I longed for an apology. My heart ached for it, but it never came. It only came when my heart was clear. It came when I forgave and released him fully to God. By the time I heard from him, I had forgiven him and he was no longer at the forefront of my thoughts. I had released him and he was a non-factor in my future due to choices he made a year earlier.

Once I seemed to gain closure, there were subtle hints of us reuniting. Eventually, the hints were not so subtle. Several months later, Doug made it very clear that he wanted to reunite. But, this time, I was prepared. I had done my self-work. I rediscovered my worth and value. In the past, I would have succumbed to his smooth, relaxed tone, which offered a temporary escape from reality. If I had fully listened, his words would have included more empty promises, more "fool's gold." After everything I allowed Doug to take me through, there was absolutely no way I could or would go back to him. Many people say, "You teach people how to treat you." I took Doug back four times, so of course he thought we would try a fifth time. Fortunately for me, this time, he encountered a 'brand new kind of me' (in the tune of Alicia Keys). He had proven, on several occasions, that neither me, nor my children, could depend on him.

So, for the first time, I told Doug, "No," and I truly meant it. I toyed with the thoughts of what could have been. I even wished he hadn't done what he did, but there was no way he could regain my trust. My heart had been through enough. I finally accepted that I deserved better than to be in a broken relationship with a man whose indecision kept me insecure and emotionally drained, even if it was my own fault for giving too much of myself. I discovered that what I needed most was consistency, dependability and true commitment. Doug could have changed. But, a year is not enough time to change in the ways in which Doug needed to change.

I couldn't risk hurting myself or my children again. It was time to cut all hopes of a healthy relationship and marriage with Doug totally off and move on. Yes, it would have been easy for us to fall back into our old roles. We'd built relationships with each other's families and friends. Breaking up with Doug was like a second divorce, but the wisdom I earned through my heartbreak and tears shaped me into who I am today. I've come too far to even attempt to look back. We just were not meant to be and that's okay. We learned the lessons from each other that we, as soul mates, were meant to teach one another and then it was time for us to move on in opposite directions.

Now that emotions are clear we chat from time to time. One day, we might even be friends. But, for now, it's best we remain associates. Now that we're apart, we're both doing better at accomplishing our individual goals. He's gone back to school to further his technology skills, and he has a position that challenges him. I'm finally writing, speaking and publishing, which I've wanted to do for years. Our individual dreams and goals are finally coming to fruition.

I also had to forgive my friends. Although many of them warned me to focus on myself and to steer clear of Doug after the first break up. Nothing could prepare me for what happened on New Year's Eve 2015. Unfortunately for me, our circle of friends was small and, although they weren't necessarily happy with him, they were tired of seeing me be a glutton for punishment. In some ways, they hoped this would be the blow that I needed to finally move on with my life. They were right. I'm grateful for everything that happened because, now, I get to shine in the light of God's redemption in clear victory of my past. I finally learned the lessons. God will do what He has to do to teach His children important lessons. I had to learn a harsh lesson on several levels. However, the biggest lesson of all was learning to be obedient to His Spirit when He speaks. I hit rock bottom. But God built me back to wholeness—layer by layer, bit by bit, tear by tear. For that, I am truly grateful.

Step 4: Let Go. Letting go wasn't as easy as I thought, but it was necessary. It began with me painfully releasing our mutual friends temporarily so that I could heal. I had to save myself. My best friend was married to his best friend, so I was dealing in very close quarters. She and I used to talk on the phone every day, several times a day before the final breakup. After that last go-round, and the painful experience right after it ended, talking to her only opened old wounds. When she called, I talked for a second, but quickly came up with an excuse to end the conversation. It was just too painful. Like most women our age, our conversations typically centered around our children, our relationships and our jobs. While I could easily discuss my children and my job, my relationship had ended with a shocking finale. The last thing I wanted or needed was a reminder. I needed to grow and I needed to heal. I couldn't do that by staying close to anyone who had a close relationship with him.

Doug's sister-in-law, "Deena," and I had developed a totally separate friendship, independent of him. Nevertheless, the pain was too great. I couldn't talk with her much either. My friend, "Cassandra," had always been very practical about things. Although she hoped Doug would get it together, she was always honest with me. One time, she told me, "Lisa, I have no doubt that you will come into your season when you release Doug and you will have love, too. But, it ain't Doug." That was very hard to hear, but she was right.

The writing had been splattered on the wall for everyone

in our circle of friends, except me. I wanted to 'drink the Kool-Aid' of my imagination, but that's the only place where my future with Doug existed. The only friend out of that circle with whom I grew closer during that time was "Danine." Danine was a vocalist like me, a true powerhouse and choir director. One day, after chatting through my pain and tears, she suggested that I join her and her music partner to sing at nursing homes. She encouraged my heart and said, "God will bless you if you use your gifts to bless other people." She was right. In my heart, I was still a church girl. I knew God had given me this voice, and I needed to use it. After several rehearsals, we encouraged the elderly at the nursing homes, and even at a church. Singing with Danine's group was truly a blessing. God used Danine to help me find my musical voice again. Through that experience, I also discovered my then five-year-old daughter's voice. She is a powerhouse in the making.

Over time, most of those friendships have been restored, but they are different. Some turned out to be seasonal or situational, and I am okay with that. It was all for the best. Of course, it hurt my friends when I pulled away; however, after several conversations and a generous helping of mutual forgiveness, pretty much everyone understood.

Step 5: Monitored My Senses. Another important step I took was to monitor my senses. I monitored what I saw, what I heard and what I felt. Although it was extremely difficult, I paid close attention to everything I watched on television and everything I listened to on the radio. I was cognizant of my myself at all times. After the New Year's fiasco, it seemed like everywhere I turned, I saw things that reminded me of Doug. Whether I saw commercials promoting engagement, television shows, or even books and magazines that I read—I saw Doug. Not only did I monitor what I listened to, but I watched the conversations I entertained as well. As a sales representative, I'm pretty much in and out of my car all day, therefore I fed my mind positivity all day. I consistently tuned into T.D. Jakes, Joel Osteen, Joyce Meyer or any other minister that had a word of encouragement for my heart. Listening to those anointed ministers, it was very easy to cut it short with friends on the phone. I wanted and needed emotional healing.

I had to monitor my emotions very carefully. I only did

what made me feel good. If it felt awkward or uncomfortable, I moved on to something else immediately. If I felt down, I got up and moved. If I felt upbeat, I did what I needed to do to stay in that mode. I was on my way up and could not afford to risk my "recovery" on unproductive emotions any longer. God held my future, and I needed to stay positive. I had to stay in faith not only to receive, but also show God that I trusted Him. I wanted healing. I was ready to move on to that good place inside of me.

Step 6: Sought Help. Depression is one of the silent killers in black communities all over the country. It kills goals, dreams, plans, marriages and careers. Sometimes, it takes lives. Nevertheless, there is still a huge stigma associated with discussing depression in the black community. Black people, in general, don't talk about depression or other mental impairments. If a woman is experiencing symptoms of depression, such as crying or not wanting to get out of bed, she's considered weak and lazy. For black men, it isn't much different. They are often told to, "Man up!" and take care of their business.

Black people live by a different code. We judge one

another and are judged by different societal rules. If you don't believe me, all you need to do is look at the evening news. Story after story depicts black men and women in stereotypical ways that don't always give authentic diverse representations of our culture. We are not monolithic, as media messages often depict. Black people were historically caregivers for others. They were not allowed to take care of themselves. However, having worked in the pharmaceutical sales industry almost twenty years, and with almost five of those years spent learning and promoting a product for mental disorders, I learned the importance of getting the appropriate support and medication when you're suffering from a mental disorder.

I started out with my primary care physician. I informed her of what I was experiencing and she placed me on Prozac. Next, through the recommendation of a friend, I sought help through the Emotional Polarity Technique. Even though traditional therapists don't acknowledge it as therapy, it served as therapy for me. In my opinion, it is literally years of traditional therapy in one hour. I learned through EPT that a lot of my issues not only stemmed from childhood, but were passed on genetically from my parents. From the first session, when I had my initial breakthrough, to my most recent session, I have continually grown and healed from past traumatic experiences. I highly recommend EPT to anyone who is serious about emotional healing. It's a great start to move forward. If you or someone you know is interested, check out gutfeelingworks.com.

As mentioned earlier, I started following my life coach, Angel Richards, while I sat heartbroken at my aunt and uncle's home in North Carolina. Eventually, I joined Angel's Clutter Free Society group and hired her as my life coach. This was another God-ordained, divine relationship. Angel, like Chanelle, was another key to get me unstuck. I was living again. Through Angel, I executed the plans and goals for my life. It was further confirmed through my vision board that I created with my Sister Circle in January of 2016.

In the session, I placed pictures on my vision board that represented areas in my life that I wanted to focus on. They included: faith, fitness, femininity, family and finances. I chose faith as an area of focus because I needed to restore my relationship with God. I needed to put Him first. I had been fully disobedient to Him when I remained in those toxic relationships. I knew full well that God was telling me to let go. Furthermore, I was hurting, and I knew that God was the only one who could heal me.

I put fitness and femininity on the board because I needed to get back in shape. I love to work out, and I love the results of higher confidence that comes from a nicely toned body. I also appreciate the lightened mood and energy boost that comes from the increased endorphin levels. I added femininity because I wanted to heal without bitterness creeping into my heart. I also wanted my sweet, soft nature to return. It had been hardened by years of too much pain. For that to happen, I had to take responsibility for my part in my heartbreak. After the second breakup with Doug, I was breaking my own heart. He had already shown me who he was, but I truly didn't want to believe him. As a result, there were not only two more heartbreaks, but they cut deeper and deeper each time. Thankfully, because I made myself my primary focus, and chose to operate in kindness and embrace my own feminine power of love and softness, I was healed, whole and feminine.

The final area was finances. When I was depressed I barely got out of bed daily to make it to work. Then, after work, I had to take care of my children. After I made sure they're needs were met, I went to bed. I paid the bills I remembered to pay and the others went to the wayside. It wasn't like I wasn't making money. My money management was off track because my mental processes were steeped in depression.

I was finally forced into reality when I arrived home from work one day and my water was off. That was my wake-up call. I knew I had to get myself together. I had plenty of money in the bank, yet one of my most important foundational bills wasn't paid. No man was worth that. I deserved better. Again, God knew how to get my attention. I went online to have my water services restored. Then, I packed the kids up and we stayed overnight at my mother's home. The next morning, I called my doctor, set a same-day appointment, and was placed on Prozac for depression. That was also when I hired my EPT therapist and got serious about moving forward with my life. The vision board I created in January was symbolic of the work that was in process, which I needed to continue. The following week,

Angel Richards announced her next coaching series, "Get in Formation," which focused on faith, fitness and finances, among other areas. It was a timely parallel, but that's how God works. He sent me confirmation. Ever since I've been working with Angel, I've been on a consistent track of setting and accomplishing goals.

Angel also recommended that I follow Tressa Azarel Smallwood and Tiphani Montgomery's former program, The BestSeller's Project. Through this course, I became unstuck as a writer and finally completed a fiction novel that I started over thirteen years ago. Since then, Tressa has become a true teacher and mentor, and I am continually inspired by her through her VIP program and other projects in which I participate.

Step 7: Intentionally Loved Myself. I loved myself intentionally. If it wasn't good for me, I didn't want or need it. Where before I spent extra time and money buying knickknacks for the kids, I started buying items for myself. I experienced things hadn't experienced in years, and I even changed my hairstyle. I got my first wavy crotchet weave, which my sister Bayle styled and cut it into a stylish bob. In addition, I scheduled a makeover at Sephora. The makeup artist did an amazing job. I purchased a beautiful plum lip color, which I still use today. I even went to a local upscale salon for additional waxes. Not only did I get my first underarm, chin and bikini wax, but, the following week, I treated myself to the ever painful, elusive, Brazilian wax. I did all of that for myself, not a man. I needed to treat myself well. In the midst of taking care of everyone else, I had forgotten to take care of myself. I had to learn to be gentle and kind to myself again, and to keep myself present in my self-care, including my thoughts.

By nature, I'm a giver. In fact, I give above and beyond and often overcommit. However, I am now consciously aware of when and what I give, both materially and not, including my time. I am careful not to give so much of myself away, especially emotionally. There are takers who would gladly use my talent, skills, money and time, and leave me depleted, those people I keep distant. Now, before I invest my time or talent in anything, I make sure that it not only adds value to my life, but that it also provides a level of fulfillment. I learned to say, "No" without feeling guilty, therefore, I liberated myself.

Step 8: Remembered Who I Was. Another pivotal point was when I remembered who I was; I came to myself. God did not create me to be small. But for a moment, I forgot that. In all of life's circumstances, and my continued self-betrayal, I lost my identity. However, even though I didn't know myself in that stage, fortunately there were people around me who reminded me from time to time. It was as though they could see the magic in me when I couldn't see it myself. I will never forget the day my younger sister Sheri said to me, in frustration, "You need to get it together. I can't remember the last time I saw you empowered." My cousin Stacy reminded me also, on more than one occasion, "You need to go back up on your ex-husband's porch and pick yourself up! You left her there." Finally, in one of my first sessions with Chanelle, my EPT practitioner, she said, "God did not create you to be small." Her intuitive nature always causes me to gawk at her accuracy.

I looked at old pictures of myself, trying to reflect and define the moment where I got lost. So much had changed in my life because of my decisions, but I knew I had to find a way back to myself. Thankfully, God granted me another opportunity to move forward in my purpose.

I paid close attention to the headshots I took in 2003, when I was planning to move to New York to get back into entertainment. I looked closely at my eyes, which were full of life, hope and naivety. I focused on my eyebrows above them, which were naturally arched thanks to my paternal genetics. I looked at my smile, the smile that came so naturally that it exuded the inner happiness I shared effortlessly. I looked at the contour of my head, the perfect oval. My lips were shaped as if they were drawn onto my face. I rediscovered my beauty. I was, I am, beautiful. But, I forgot for a moment. How could I have let anyone's rejection, man or woman, make me feel so ugly and unworthy? Never again would I allow anyone that kind of power over my life. Only God would lead my decisions. I am a child of God; therefore, I am worthy of all that is good. It is my birthright.

Step 9: I Moved Forward. As I regained focus, I learned to put myself first. I became happier day by day. It took a lot of time and energy to get to a place of wholeness, but I did it. I prayed constantly, and I did the work. I started from a place of devastation, but every ounce of pain I felt was worth it. I spent thirteen years off track from my purpose. From late fall 2003 until the spring of 2016, I felt totally lost.

However, when God gave me the gift of man's betrayal, He allowed the pain to take me to my lowest point; it was there that I learned to only depend on God. It was through this heartache that God built me back stronger and He helped me bounce back. Through God I learned to set standards in relationships, and to live by them, anything less is a deal breaker. It's okay to compromise activities and actions in relationships; but never at the expense of your identity. If you're a star, be a star and don't let your voice be silenced. If you're a dancer and you like to dance, don't stop dancing because someone else doesn't like it, be your authentic self and live in that space. If your partner doesn't like it or tries to limit your ability to do what you love, perhaps that's not the appropriate partner for you. Love yourself and live true to yourself, that is the space in which you will thrive.

Perhaps you have spent many years lost because of self-betrayal, either by walking away from your purpose, giving too much or overcommitting. Maybe you are a woman who is in a season of transition. Maybe you've experienced loss due to man's betrayal, divorce or the death of a loved one. Perhaps you have experienced depression, or maybe you're simply seeking the tools to help you find your purpose.

Whatever the case, at whatever stage you find yourself, rest assured that God will get you through if you do the work and have faith.

The following workbook will provide you with introspective questions that will serve as tools to help you delve deep inside to analyze your past, present and future. Applying these tools will boost your confidence as you begin your journey back to self and experience your own BounceBack.

The BounceBack Workbook

A Guide to Jumpstart Women Back to Themselves

As women, we juggle multiple roles daily, often at one time, putting on a new persona as the job demands. We go from wife, to mom, to co-worker, then to volunteer and lover—often all in the same day and, in many cases, within a few hours. We work hard to accommodate others. Oftentimes, we mistake our "busyness" for purpose and life fulfillment. We put ourselves on the backburner while we serve and support the dreams and visions of others around us.

It is only when we slow down and take time to reflect that we re-discover our identity. Below is a list of questions that are designed for you to take the masks off and look deeply at your life. Do you know who you are? Are you living the life God designed for you, or are you merely coping in a lifestyle someone else imposed upon you? Have you ever taken time to explore your life at all? It is my hope that by going through this guide, you will not only discover yourself, but also, upon completion that you will have a plan to move you forward in your journey authentically. You will also be clear about who you are, apart from the daily masks you've worn in the past. From that space, you will have the tools to build your life being more of your authentic self.

As you move forward, if you have any questions, concerns or feedback, feel free to reach out to me at lisabethwillis. com or at bouncebackworkshop@gmail.com. You can also follow me on Instagram, Twitter, Facebook or at my blog bouncebacktips.com.

Are you ready to begin your journey? Let's go!

The BounceBack Workbook is divided into two sections. At any given point in life, an individual may experience something from which they need to recover. The first section is for the woman who has lost her purpose and is seeking identity. If this is you, these questions solely focus on the helping you find yourself and finding your life's purpose. The second section is focused on bouncing back from divorce or heartbreak. In this section, I lead you through a series of steps that mimic my own experience to usher you back to your own authentic happiness.

Rediscovering Your Identity & Purpose

Who are you?

(Not what you do. Who are you as an individual?)

Are you happy with your life and who you are as an individual? Why or

why not?

....

....

....

Who and what did you dream of being when you grew up?

....

....

....

Did those dreams transition into goals?

....

....

....

Are you living the life of your dreams? Why or why not? What happened

to "her" dreams?

....

....

....

How and when did you change? What deterred you from your dreams?

....

....

....

What factors are inhibiting you from becoming the woman of your

dreams?

....

....

....

Have you forgiven yourself for not becoming the woman you dreamed

you would be by now?

....

....

....

If others are involved, have you forgiven them for the role they played in

you not achieving your dreams?

....

....

....

Are there extenuating circumstances that are holding you back?

....

....

....

Do you need to hire professional help to get on track? If so, what type?

....

....

....

Do you have a mentor or life coach to guide you? Do you need an accountability partner?

....

....

....

Do you need to separate yourself from certain people? Are they toxic to who you want to become?

....

....

....

Do you need to limit or change your habits like limiting TV radio to clear your thoughts? Do you meditate or sit in silence?

....

....

....

What are your current goals? Professionally and personally?

....

....

....

List three action steps you can take to move you forward.

....

....

....

Do you need to discuss your transition into the "authentic you" with anyone? What will you say? How will your transformation affect them?

....

....

....

What, if anything, are you risking by transitioning into the "authentic you"?

....

....

....

What do you risk by staying the same?

....

....

....

How many hours a day can you commit to your journey?

....

....

....

What can you do to ensure that your BounceBack is authentic and

continues? How will you maintain consistency?

....

....

....

What are three action steps that you can take today to ensure that you

are consistent?

....

....

....

Bouncing Back from Heartbreak and/or Divorce

The end of a serious relationship or marriage is one of the most traumatic experiences an individual might ever encounter. Regardless of the reasons for the divorce, it is sometimes "natural" for one or both partners to attempt to assign blame. However, if you truly want to expedite the healing process and recover, without grudges and/or bitterness, you must focus on yourself and forgiveness. You must forgive yourself first, then forgive the other individual, whether they are sorry or not. This is about your own peace of mind and spirit. Most of all, it's about regaining wholeness to move forward.

Who are you and what type of person are you today?

Did you become someone different in your relationship? Why? Were these changes influenced by your mate or someone else?

....

....

....

How are you different from the woman you were when you entered your relationship/marriage?

....

....

....

Did you love yourself at the beginning of your relationship? Did you or do you love the woman you became while you were in your relationship?

....

....

....

Were you happy and did you feel whole when you entered the relationship? Why or why not?

....

....

Did you feel happy and whole during the relationship? Why or why not?

....

....

....

Why did your relationship end?

....

....

....

Did you want your relationship to end? Why or why not?

....

....

....

What role did you play in the relationship ending?

....

....

....

Did you stay in that relationship/marriage too long? Did you know in your heart it was over? Why or why not?

....

....

....

Was your intuition speaking to you regarding your relationship? Spiritually, did you know it was time for your relationship to end? Did you resist?

....

....

....

Did you trust and follow your intuition? Why or why not?

....

....

....

What was the result of you following (or not following) your intuition? If you were disobedient, what was the price you paid for it? If you were obedient, have you yet discovered your reward?

....

....

....

If your mate asked, would you go back to him? Why or why not?

....

....

....

If you answered yes to the question above, is it because you are seeking to

fill a void?

....

....

....

Do you understand that God made you whole at birth, and man was not

created to fulfill a void inside of you? (While a man may fit your outward

vision for your life, he cannot fill your spirit).

....

....

....

Have you determined how to move forward? If so, what are the next

steps? If not, began to contemplate a strategy to move you forward.

Your Strategy:

....

....

....

Have you prayed about your situation? If you ignored your intuition/ inward spirit, have you asked God for forgiveness? Have you asked God for restoration and guidance? If not, do so now.

....

....

....

Have you forgiven yourself? If not, look in the mirror and, with your heart, say aloud, "I forgive me." (Meditate on two songs: "Mirror" by Lalah Hathaway and "I Forgive Me" by James Fortune)

....

....

....

Have you forgiven your former mate? Why or why not? Do you understand that forgiveness is a direct path to healing? Understand that you may not 'feel' that you forgive him in your heart or mind, but say it anyway. Eventually, it will become real to you. This step must become an applied mandate in every area of life. The Bible instructs that we must forgive as Christ has forgiven us.

....

....

....

....

....

....

....

....

....

Do you understand that it's time to let go? That means to release the need to "own" your place in his life. In addition, return any items that belong to him. Put away or hide any items that remind you of him, if you choose to keep them. How will you begin the process of letting go?

....

....

....

What mutual friends do you need to release temporarily?

....

....

....

How is your mindset? Naturally, you may not be in the best emotional state while you're in the healing process. Monitor your senses. What are you listening to daily? Is it music that brings you down instead of inspiring you? What are your phone calls with friends like? Do you need to limit conversations with friends that remind you of your pain or former mate? What type of words are you speaking to yourself about yourself? What type of words are coming out of your mouth to others? Do you discuss your former mate? If so, stop immediately. If you slip, forgive yourself and move forward. List these answers in detail. More space is allowed for this section.

....

....

....

....

....

....

....

....

....

....

....

....

....

Do you need professional help? Are you experiencing depression? If so, do not hesitate to seek help from your physician. You may temporarily need to be be placed on medication. Perhaps seeking traditional therapy with a psychologist will help. I have done both. However, I have also experienced what I call 'alternative therapy' through the Emotional Polarity Technique. I can attest that they all have worked for me.

....

....

....

....

....

Do you love yourself? If so, what action can you take daily to intentionally show yourself love? (I recently heard Sarah Jakes Roberts say that, "By continuing to place ourselves in situations that continually break us or hurt us, we may not be loving ourselves like we need to."

Please keep this in mind when creating your list.) Only do what uplifts your spirit and makes you feel whole.

....

....

....

....

....

What type of woman do you want to become? How is she different from who you were before your relationship? What steps can you take daily to become her? You move forward by focusing on yourself and doing those things that create the life you desire. Have you established new standards for your life? If so, what are they? What are your deal breakers? Remember, do not compromise on any standard that is directly related to your identity.

....

....

....

....

....

Do you have a vision board? If not, create one. If you don't know how to begin, research on the internet. Many sites offer tips on creating vision boards.

....

....

....

....

....

Do you need a life coach? At this stage in my life, I do not consider myself a coach. However, I highly recommend them. Research life coaches and ask God to lead you to the one that is right for you. Keep an open mind. Interview them as a candidate (as most are not free), then choose the one who speaks to you and your life experiences. There should be a connection with you and your coach. If there isn't an authentic connection, look for someone else. Use this space to list names of potential candidates.

....

....

....

....

....

CONCLUSION

It is my sincere hope that, by going through the processes of healing outlined in this workbook, you found guidance to move forward to the next phase in your life. In addition, please remember that self-work is life-work. It is never one and done. Continue to seek God, live true to yourself authentically, and always hold yourself in the highest regard. If for some reason you go off course, or even get lost, know that God is still carrying you and you can always bounce back. The BounceBack Workbook is a guide to jumpstart you on your journey; however, healing and growth will only occur if you do the work of applying the knowledge you've gained. Continue to seek God's blessings upon your life as He blesses you on your BounceBack.

Epilogue

Thank you for your support of The BounceBack: From Heartbreak to Wholeness. It is my hope that this memoir and workbook provided you with the exact information you need to move forward. As women, it is very easy to lose ourselves by giving too much of ourselves away. If you allow, The BounceBack: From Heartbreak to Wholeness can serve as a tool to guide you to becoming whole, without bitterness and regret. It will also inform you of the dangers of not following your intuition and ignoring the nudges from God as He speaks. As the late Maya Angelou stated, "We are more alike than we are different." So, I know there are many women who have experienced much of what I share. Be blessed and remember to always BounceBack.

About the Author

LisaBeth Willis is a multi-talented author and speaker from Ohio. She is the mother of two children and holds both a bachelor's and master's degree. The BounceBack: From Heartbreak to Wholeness is the first book publication of her company, Abounding Phoenix Publishing, LLC. She can be followed on her website lisabethwillis.com, Twitter, Instagram and Facebook.

www.ingramcontent.com/pod-product-compliance
Lightning Source LLC
LaVergne TN
LVHW021505080426
835509LV00018B/2402